The ABC of Work Motivation

The ABC of Work Motivation

How to Energize Any Organization

Anja Van den Broeck,
Hermina Van Coillie,
Jacques Forest, and
Marcus B. Müller

Amsterdam University Press

Cover design: Eric Guémise, Freelance Motion Graphics/Coördesign, Leiden
Lay-out: Crius Group, Hulshout

ISBN 978 90 4856 273 2
e-ISBN 978 90 4856 274 9
NUR 801

Printed and bound by CPI Group (UK) Ltd, Croydon, CR0 4YY

Table of contents

PART 2 TOOLS TO START WORKING WITH SELF-DETERMINATION THEORY

Foreword

Enhancing the motivation of employees is a key objective in most modern organizations. Engagement is easy to measure and even easier to observe. Spend some time within a company, and you'll notice that the level of involvement is generally palpable. You can feel it in the enthusiasm with which people approach their tasks and in their energy when interacting with colleagues. In an environment where individuals are invested, camaraderie is powerful, and there is a sense of purpose and a concern for the quality of services or products. Disengagement is equally striking: morale is low, emotions are negative, and everyone is simply waiting for the weekend.

While engagement and disengagement are thus evident, it is not always easy to change them. The latest data from major corporations show that, despite massive expenditures on employee motivation initiatives, the average engagement rate has decreased post-pandemic. In this time of turbulence, many good workers have even questioned their relationship with their jobs and started seeking a new vocation where they can find more meaning and a form of fulfillment beyond just a paycheck.

This trend urges leaders worldwide to pay more attention to factors that can help their employees be more involved, satisfied, and perform better. Fortunately, new developments in the science of motivation allow us to identify reliable paths to improve well-being and productivity. In particular, Self-Determination Theory (SDT) provides a revolutionary perspective that emphasizes individuals' quality of motivation and psychological needs. This theory explains in detail how management styles, work climate, and job design can address psychological needs at all levels of the organization, fostering increased engagement, effort, and quality production. SDT shows notably that when managers adopt leadership styles that support autonomy, belongingness, and competence, both their subordinates and the organization benefit. Not only is there more motivation and well-being, but also better results. Another positive side effect is that managers themselves are more satisfied when they adopt such leadership strategies.

This brings us to the importance and uniqueness of this book, written by four experts in Self-Determination Theory and organizational behavior. Informed by the latest motivation research and their respective consulting experiences, this work synthesizes theory and observations, making them applicable by presenting the pillars of motivation and well-being. The authors emphasize practical measures that can catalyze more vitality and satisfaction in everyday work. They provide concrete examples and compelling case studies from various sectors and organizations. More uniquely, this book not only addresses how managers can help employees but also what employees can do for themselves to improve their own motivation and professional fulfillment. It thus provides the means to cultivate intrinsic motivation and meaning, both for others and oneself.

As a co-founder of SDT, I am delighted to present this work. The main reason we continuously develop, test, and refine psychological theories is that we are trying to "change the world" and steer it in a better direction. This is why it seems so important to start with workplaces, where we, as adults, invest so much of our energy, and whose conditions profoundly impact our quality of life and mental health, both during and outside the hours we spend there. In this regard, it is inspiring to see organizational research on SDT from a global community of scholars being applied so practically in this book. Its reading provides reasons to reflect, ideas for innovation, and a compass to find our way towards greater well-being at work, in our relationships, and in life in general.

Richard M. Ryan, Ph.D.
co-founder of SDT

Preface

To motivate people or "to get them to move" is quite an art. Often we want to motivate others. **Anja** for example wants to motivate herself to do her work with passion (without becoming addicted to it) and to eat fewer cookies. She also wants to motivate her husband to take that big trip to Australia, and her students to read books and immerse themselves in their study materials (instead of taking the easy route to studying).

Hermina wants to motivate her four children to clean up their room (not easy), read books (instead of comics), study (not easy at all), and eat vegetables (much easier said than done). And not only when they are with her, but also when they go camping with their sports club when she can't motivate them with a dessert. She also wants to motivate herself to walk every week and to eat a yoghurt in the evening instead of a bag of chips.

Jacques wants his two children to learn the beauty of discipline by having fun and finding things important, especially when it comes to school, sport activity and eating. He also wants his students to find their "true" self so that motivation comes mostly from within. On a personal note, he wants to eat more healthy and balance the numerous challenges of his different roles: father, husband, psychologist, cyclist, professor, skier, friend, etc.

Marcus' mission in life is to motivate people to change their own lives and contribute to the lives of others – for the better! The ABC has changed his life. In turn, he has been applying the ABC framework to help create health, well-being and success for his family, friends, colleagues, students, clients, communities and society at large.

Our professional careers brought us to Self-Determination Theory and – thanks to the theory – we found each other.

Self-Determination Theory (SDT) is a recent theory of motivation that assumes that people naturally have the energy to be motivated. And that they are not only motivated "a lot" but especially "well", i.e., that their motivation is of high quality.

When we want to motivate people, SDT says, there is no need to threaten them with a stick, entice them with a carrot or continuously control them. To the contrary! If you control people too much, their motivation and energy slip away like sand between your fingers: the harder you squeeze, the more sand slips away, until eventually you are left empty-handed.

Rather than being controlling, we can motivate ourselves and others without putting pressure. SDT helps to do exactly that, also in the workplace. Every job has some tasks that are less pleasant, for which people are not intrinsically motivated. In this book we bring forward the basics of SDT and we indicate how SDT helps you to have high-quality motivation which helps to make that impossible deadline, get your employees to go along with the organizational change and encourage your boss to bring more structure to meetings. SDT indicates how relationships in the workplace, compensation, jobs, and the organizational climate can be motivating. It accomplishes this through the ABC of motivation and by eliciting high-quality motivation, that is, through internal drive instead of outside control.

We have deliberately chosen to keep the book short and added questions and exercises for yourself and your team to make it more practical. We also bring a number of examples from our consultation practices. In this way we hope to inspire and inform you. We also hope that you, perhaps together with your colleagues or managers, will become inspired to apply SDT in your workplace.

We hope you enjoy reading it and look forward to helping you motivate yourself and others at work!

Anja, Hermina, Jacques, and Marcus

1. WHY MOTIVATE ACCORDING TO SELF-DETERMINATION THEORY?

WHAT MOTIVATES YOU FOR YOUR WORK? AND HOW DO YOU MOTIVATE OTHERS?

- Do you think your boss is controlling you?
- Do you enjoy doing all your tasks?
- Do you explain why a (tedious) task is important?
- Do you ever use the word "have to" or similar expressions in your instructions ("you have to do this", "you must do that")?
- Do you let others be themselves at work?
- Do you enjoy receiving a bonus?
- Do you trust all your colleagues?

All of these questions have to do with motivation at work.

1.1 Without motivation there is no behavior

The word "motivation" comes from the Latin "movere" (to move).

Motivation is the energy:
- that makes you choose this task or another;
- that sets you in motion;
- that makes you persevere, even when the going gets tough.

In short, without motivation there is no movement. It is the basis of everything we do. Motivation helps you to do your job, to work hard. Or to avoid certain tasks.

Your motivation, for example, gives you the energy to finish the marketing campaign for that one client. It helps you persist in writing a book, even when it becomes difficult. It makes you doodle on your smartphone instead of actively participating in a meeting. Who or what motivates you in those moments may vary. But there's no question that "something" is causing you to do the things you do. Without the drive or motivation for your work, you may sit in front of the TV with a bag of chips (or with something healthier if you are motivated to eat healthy). Motivation drives your behavior and gets you moving. Without motivation there is no behavior.

Given the importance of motivation, it may not come as a surprise that the academic literature has extensively studied how we can best "motivate" and "set in motion" ourselves and others. There are many theories about motivation, including widely known theories such as Maslow's "pyramid of needs" (which never got scientifically validated as a true pyramid), or Bandura's "self-efficacy theory", saying that people are primarily motivated by what they think they are good at. Also "goal-setting theory" and its derivate of "management by objectives" are often used in practice. They assume that people are mostly motivated when they set difficult but achievable goals.

Self-Determination Theory (SDT) is a recent, yet thoroughly tested theory. Its foundation was laid in the 1970s, but over the years, it has evolved into the rich theory that it is today. We have chosen to base this book in SDT.

1.2   SDT is one of the most influential motivation theories

SDT is very valuable for several reasons, especially in the workplace.

First, to date, SDT has become one of the most prominent, well-established, and innovative theories of motivation. The theory originates from the 1970s when one of its "founding fathers," Edward Deci, conducted experiments on the impact of rewards on intrinsic motivation (doing something out of interest or enjoyment). By now, thanks to an ever-growing academic community around the world, SDT has grown into a broad theory and movement. Thousands of academic and peer reviewed articles and books have been published on this theory.

Second, SDT is a universal theory: whether you are trying to boost yourself for that important deadline, trying to get your coworker to pull out a new project, trying to motivate your partner to put their socks in the laundry or to motivate your child to do their homework, the principles of SDT help with all those motivation issues. The same motivation principles are thus not only valid in the workplace, but also at home, in the gym and in the classroom. And not only in the Western world, but all across the globe.

Third, SDT is a broad theory. SDT says something about why we do what we do and where we get our energy from. SDT also indicates for whom the theory works and how we can strengthen high-quality motivation.

Employees or executives who receive an introduction or training based on this theory often see it as a gift. Investing in the basic principles of SDT not only helps in one's personal relations but also benefits the organization. Research indicates that investing in SDT reduces the risk of burnout within the organization and helps employees to be more productive and innovative. It also ensures that employees feel more involved with their organization, perform better and are less absent. Research shows that every dollar invested in improving employee motivation according to the principles of SDT, pays back more than threefold within 12 months.

SDT also deflates some classic myths surrounding motivation, such as:

A) Some employees cannot be motivated
SDT starts from the positive view that *everyone* is motivated, even your most difficult coworker. Of course, not everyone is always equally motivated, and maybe not motivated for a particular task, but you can increase the quality of everyone's motivation. However, improving people's motivation is not likely to be achieved through money, control, or threat of punishment. The right approach is needed: it is important to create the right environment in which your employees can and want to give the best of themselves. SDT offers concrete ways of achieving this. The advantage of using the SDT approach is that you do not constantly have to monitor and control others. Within the right circumstances employees will motivate themselves.

B) Intrinsic motivation is best
According to SDT, intrinsic motivation is not the holy grail of motivation. People are intrinsically motivated if they like doing a task because it is fun or interesting. However, in life in general and at work in particular there is more than only fun things to do. Also tasks and projects that are less enjoyable and pleasant are on your plate. Does this mean that people cannot be motivated for those? Not at all. SDT makes it clear that when you make these tasks meaningful and important, people can be motivated to perform them just as well as if you had found them fun or enjoyable from the outset, even when they are not intrinsically motivated to engage in them.

C) *The more motivation, the better*

Employees can be motivated in different ways for their work. They may find their work engaging, fun, or valuable. But of course, people can also do things out of external or internal pressure: because others force them to engage in these behaviors or because they would otherwise feel bad about themselves or guilty. Obviously, fear or guilt are less qualitative forms of motivation. So SDT argues that "more motivation" is not always "better" and helps to encourage the right types of motivation. When employees have high-quality motivation, they feel good at work and give their best.

D) *Motivating your employees is hard and complex*

Although SDT can sometimes seem complex, it also provides a handy ABC to work with in practice. SDT argues that employees are optimally motivated and have lots of energy when they experience (A) autonomy, (B) belongingness, and (C) competence at work. This ABC can help you, for example, to motivate others using the right communication, designing the right compensation systems, jobs or leadership styles. In this way SDT helps you to create the necessary circumstances in which employees not only have any type of motivation but especially "optimal" or high-quality motivation.

"Instead of asking, "How can I motivate people", we should be asking, "How can I create the conditions within which people will motivate themselves?""

EDWARD DECI

Because SDT is such a rich and exciting theory that helps to motivate, in this book, we tell you exactly what it entails and how you can get started with it. We start with its basic assumptions. We look at the types of motivation that SDT puts forward and talk about its ABC. We then clarify how high-quality motivation can come about in the work context. We furthermore discuss for whom the theory works (spoiler alert: for (almost) everyone), and then detail the importance of a fair, just and transparent compensation system, the design of jobs, the impact of colleagues and customers, and conclude with leadership. The figure below provides an overview.

Work Environment

Organizational climate
Reward policy
Job design
Leadership
Colleagues/clients
Communication

Employee

Individual differences
Mindfulness
Values
Culture

Basic needs

Autonomy
Belongingness
Competence

Motivations

Not motivated
External pressure
Internal pressure
Meaningfulness
Pleasure/ interest

Optional functioning of the employee

Performance
Wellbeing
Emotions Health
Stress / burnout

Organizational Outcomes

Sales
Clients

PART 1

THE PRINCIPLES OF
SELF-DETERMINATION THEORY

1. THE METATHEORY OF SDT: WHAT YOU THINK IS WHAT YOU GET

HOW DO YOU FEEL ABOUT YOUR COLLEAGUES AND/OR EMPLOYEES?

- Are they lazy, easily tired and do they lack motivation for their work?
- Do you regularly have to check if they are really at work?
- Do you often have to check them closely to see if they are doing their job?

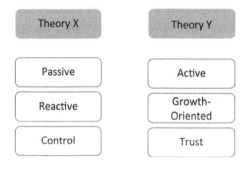

1.1 Theory X and Y: a different view of people

A) Theory X: a pessimistic view of employees
Do you assume that people are rather passive and lazy? Little or not at all motivated for work by nature? That – just like on a lazy Sunday – people would rather sleep long and just languish? Do you think that people need a lot of pressure to do something? And a lot of control?

If you have this view, then you are more likely to see the world through the lens of Theory X, as McGregor pointed out in 1960.

Managers with a Theory X perspective assume that their employees do not want to devote time and energy to their work and only take action when they really have to. Such a view is also shared in Agency Theory, which states that "agents" (e.g., company executives and employees) are relatable to "principals" (e.g., shareholders, company owners).

From that point of view, employees can hardly be trusted. You constantly have to keep an eye on them and check whether they are doing their job and are doing it right. When given the opportunity, they will secretly spend hours on the toilet, waste their time on social media or, when working from home, be mostly preoccupied with private matters. According to this perspective, employees are not committed to the organization. Theory X states that employees only come to work for the paycheck. From this perspective, giving financial rewards for good work or threatening to quit when things don't go well, are good ways to motivate employees.

"Anything that is truly great and inspiring is created by the individual who can labor in freedom."

ALBERT EINSTEIN

B) Theory Y: an optimistic view of employees
Or do you assume that most employees are virtuous? That they are most likely to be active and growth-oriented? Do they have a lot of talents they want to develop? Do they want to learn? Do employees not wait passively, but look for solutions and improvements, even before the problems arise?

If this vision is more in line with how you think, then you think according to Theory Y. Managers working from a Theory Y perspective assume that employees are not passive and do not just let their actions be determined by others. Their employees are proactive and shape their environment themselves. Theory Y assumes that employees care about the organization and enjoy devoting their time and energy to their work. After all, they chose a particular profession and applied for your particular organization and not elsewhere. Working from this perspective, collaborating is based on trust. More than that: it is encouraged to give employees space to be able to give the best of themselves.

"The fact is that people are good. Give people affection and security, and they will give affection and be secure in their feelings and their behavior."

ABRAHAM MASLOW

1.2 Your way of thinking has important implications for how you motivate employees

Whether you hold a Theory X or Theory Y perspective on people may be more of an ideological choice. It is dictated by who you are, your upbringing and personal experiences. What is important, however, is that this choice determines how you deal with your employees and – consequently – how they are motivated for their work, as the quality of their motivation will drive their behavior.

If you start from a Theory X human perspective, then you will continuously give your colleagues and staff orders, closely monitor whether they do their work and give them the necessary rewards (or punishments) for when they do (not) keep in with your performance standards. Those who do a poor job will get scolded, be bypassed for promotions, or even be fired. Mistakes are punished. Those who do a good job receive praise, a bonus or are left alone. In other words, people who have a negative view of people motivate others (and themselves) using the stick, or in the best case, the carrot approach.

If you think more from a Theory Y perspective, you will motivate your coworkers and employees in a very different way. You will then not use the stick and carrot, because you assume that your employees don't need external incentives. They are already motivated. All you have to do is enable that energy to flourish to the benefit of the organization. Mistakes are seen as growth opportunities. The classic image of a donkey that needs to be pushed around, is then replaced by one that naturally likes to be on the move. As a manager, it is up to you to see, together with your employees, how you can work together to bring the organization a step closer to its goal. You then create the conditions in which employees can immerse themselves fully in their work, tasks, deadlines and projects.

1.3   You get what you think

Based on science it is impossible to tell whether Theory X or Theory Y is right. However, it does become clear that working from either Theory X or Y leads to very different results. If you assume that people are lazy and need to be controlled, people will wait for you to give the orders, because that is the most effective option to keep you satisfied as a colleague, supervisor, HR manager or consultant. Suppose they would take initiative in a direction you don't want, then they would have invested all that energy without being rewarded for it. Or worse: they are punished because they have wasted their time or are seen as troublemakers who always want to do the opposite to what they are told.

In contrast, if you think employees are active and growth-oriented, you encourage them to do their best, come up with new ideas and take action. Employees who are given such opportunities are often capable of great things.

*"If I kick my dog, he will move. And when I want him to move
again, what must I do? I must kick him again. But it is only
when he has his own generator that we can talk about motivation. He then needs no outside stimulation. He wants to do it."*

FREDRICK HERZBERG

1.4 SDT starts from Theory Y

SDT starts from the positive, Theory Y, perspective that people
are inherently active, growth-oriented and interact with their
environment. Of course, people can be passive at times. Who
doesn't like a lazy Sunday morning where you don't have to do
anything? But research shows that people who manage to appeal
to the active growth tendency of employees get proactive and
committed employees in return. There are already a number
of organizations working from a Theory Y people perspective.

Often referred to examples include online shoe and clothing store
ZAPPOS, which lets employees decorate and personalize their
workspace while hiring employees that are "fun and a little weird,"
hence boosting autonomy and relatedness. Netflix is another
example where employees can take as much vacation as they
want inasmuch as they meet their quantity and quality goals; this
boosts responsibility and self-directedness. Another interesting
case is Google with its "20% time policy", where employees can
spend 1/5 of their time working on whatever projects they want,
hence unleashing their potential and creativity.

The above examples are completely different from what happens
when you reason from Theory X, as in the following examples.

In a government department, people's authority is defined
according to their level of education. Lower-level employees
must go through the necessary procedures to get approval

from their superior, even if they have more experience and expertise.

Sonja's supervisor checks her work meticulously, providing many detailed comments. Sonja never receives constructive feedback on the broader picture.

In a construction company, employees have to use the time clock every day. For Hans, who carpools with a colleague who is often late, this is a real problem. He has already received three warnings. If he is late one more time, he will be fired, even if he and his colleague manage to deliver all the work within the agreed time frame.

Theory X and Theory Y thinking seeps into various facets of management, HR, leadership and mentoring, i.e., in motivating real people in real life. Sometimes it's in the details: Whether you work from an X or Y perspective is also reflected in the way you speak, in how you give feedback and in your tolerance toward mistakes. The basic question is: what do you think about people? And how does this trickle down into your behavior, which then influences employees? What you think determines how your employees will behave. So: what you think is what you get.

WHAT ABOUT YOU?

— Are you more likely to act from Theory X or Theory Y?
— Do you hold the same view of all your employees? Or do you have different views of different employees? In other words, do you use Theory X for some and Theory Y for others?
— Do you try to motivate different employees in different ways?

TIP

Try Theory Y even if you think Theory X would better work in your team. We often hear "SDT looks nice, but not for my team. My employees just can't be trusted, they really only work for the money". Yet this is true for only 2 to 4% of people, with underlying pathologies such as narcissistic personality disorder or psychopathy. For the remaining 96 to 98%, Theory Y thinking will work. Just give it a try. And also know that if you approach your employees from Theory X, "you will get what you think". And then Theory X will install itself effectively in your organization as well.

CASE

Peter is a controlling CEO, a micro-manager who likes to control every aspect of his employees' behavior. He rules his employees with an iron fist, gives them little autonomy and motivates them with an elaborate bonus system. "Without control they don't do anything," he says. But then Peter attends a keynote on SDT, which triggers something in him. Somehow he feels that his way of doing things does work, but mainly in the very short term, and it requires a lot of energy. He is willing to loosen the reins a bit for a team of welders. A kind of pilot project so to speak. If it would fail (and he initially estimates this chance to be very high) he can show that SDT does not work for everyone, and that Theory X is applicable to his company. He starts a nice SDT project for the team, where the focus is on autonomy, belongingness, and competence. Via workshops with concrete exercises, open conversations, empathic listening and, above all, thanks to the growing trust between Peter and the welders, everyone sees how the entire team starts to flourish. Peter can only smile when he sees he can manage this fantastic team from a Theory Y perspective. It makes his job much easier. The SDT program is subsequently successfully rolled out throughout the whole organization.

---

2. AUTONOMOUS AND CONTROLLED MOTIVATION: "I WANT TO" VERSUS "I HAVE TO" MAKES A WORLD OF DIFFERENCE

WHY ARE YOU READING THIS BOOK?

- Do you enjoy reading it, cozying up with a cup of coffee?
- Do you think it's important to educate yourself and learn new things?
- Do you feel better about yourself when you try to stay up-to-date? Or are you looking for reassurance in this book that you are doing the right thing?
- Do you want to impress your coworkers or boss, or are you hoping to get promotion when you can better motivate your employees?
- Does this book offer distraction, for example while waiting in the airport? You might as well have been doing something else.
- Do each of these reasons play a role?

People can have different reasons for doing what they do. According to SDT, these are all different types of motivation. The question then is, which types are there? And most importantly, are they all equally good?

2.1 Motivated or not?

In general, we can make a distinction between being "motivated" and being "not motivated". Some employees clearly lack motivation. We call this "amotivation". People who have no motivation feel helpless and have the feeling that taking action is futile because they won't achieve the desired outcome anyway. Employees who are not motivated for their job do show up, but they go through the day counting the hours.

Others, in contrast, do see reasons to show up for work and do their best. According to SDT, we can safely assume that most employees are motivated for their work. This is also what our research shows. Most people are motivated for their work in one way or another. What is unique about SDT is that it indicates that people can have different reasons for being motivated. And those different reasons lead to different consequences.

2.2 Types of motivation

2.2.1 Intrinsic and extrinsic

Presumably you've heard of the idea that employees can be intrinsically or extrinsically motivated.

Intrinsic motivation: When you are intrinsically motivated you enjoy your work. You find your work fascinating or experience pleasure in doing it. Even if you were to win the lottery, you would still do your job or similar tasks. For example, intrinsically motivated nurses will remain committed to helping others, e.g. by volunteering. An intrinsically motivated consultant who retires at 65 finds pleasure in continuing to advise people as a freelancer.

Extrinsic motivation: If you are extrinsically motivated you do your work to get something in return, like a paycheck, a nice company car or a pat on the back. Work in itself is not rewarding: there needs to be something external in return. You don't like the work itself and would stop as soon as possible, but stick to it while looking forward to the reward that comes by doing it.

As an employer or manager, it is not always easy to increase your employees' intrinsic motivation. You have an impact through your style of leadership and the way you shape work (explained in Part 2), but not all tasks are equally fun or exciting. Someone who is afraid of standing in front of an audience will not enjoy presenting, no matter how hard you invest in the ideal conditions. Similarly, only few employees experience joy in creating expense reports. Yet, it must be done.

Classical motivational theories highlight rewards and punishments as the best way to motivate employees in these situations. You can promise a bonus to an employee who – despite their fears – successfully holds a customer presentation. Or give someone a warning if they are late with their administration. But pushing the extrinsic motivation button to motivate someone "more" can be dangerous.

2.2.2   Interplay between intrinsic and extrinsic motivation

The research on which SDT was founded started with the fascinating dynamic between intrinsic and extrinsic motivation. In 1971, Edward Deci had two groups of students do intrinsically motivating puzzles. Each group was invited into the lab three times. First, they worked on the puzzles. Halfway through each session, Deci indicated that he needed to leave the lab for a moment to get the next trial ready. During that break, the students were allowed to do whatever they wanted: stare around, read a magazine or continue working on the puzzles. Through a one-way mirror, Deci watched whether and how long students continued to work on the puzzles. This was his measure of intrinsic motivation, as students had no other reason to work on the puzzles than the inherent pleasure they experienced in solving them.

In both the control and experimental group, the students went through this scenario. In the control group, they did puzzles three times and were given a break after each time. In the experimental group, they were given exactly the same task, but the second time they were given $1 for each completed puzzle. In this way, Deci tried to increase the students' motivation in an extrinsic way. When the students came to the lab for the third time, they were told that the money had run out and they were no longer being paid for completing the puzzles. Students thus received the same treatment in the last phase as they did in the first; which, by the way, was completely identical to the last trial of the students in the control group, who were never rewarded.

The students in the control group continued to work on the puzzles in all phases more or less for the same amount of time. But among the students in the experimental group there was a big difference in puzzle time during each of the three breaks. When they were paid in the second phase, they were clearly more motivated. They worked on the puzzles longer during the break of the second session than during the break of the first session. You would expect them to. After all, their motivation to do these puzzles was significantly greater in the second session: they were not only intrinsically motivated, but extrinsically as well.

But the single most important result of this experiment was that the students who were paid in the second session spent distinctly less time doing puzzles in the third session than in the first! In the third session, they were thus clearly less motivated. Even more: they worked on the puzzles markedly less than the control group students, who had never been paid throughout the three sessions. After receiving money in the second session, the students in the experimental group were thus less motivated in the final phase for the fun puzzles than those who had never been paid. Their extrinsic motivation (money) had – negatively – affected their intrinsic motivation.

Deci and colleagues repeated this type of experiment a few more times, both in the lab and out. Sometimes they paid their research participants. Sometimes, they gave them positive feedback as a social reward. Sometimes intrinsic motivation was assessed by looking at the participants' behavior, other times their motivation was measured through questionnaires. Each time they came to the same conclusion: those who were rewarded for an intrinsically motivating task and then saw that reward disappear, were less intrinsically motivated afterwards. The extrinsic motivation had decreased the intrinsic motivation, which is known as the *crowding out effect*.

Perhaps you have experienced this crowing out effect as well. Maybe you liked reading until you had to do mandatory book reviews in secondary school? Or maybe you were able to turn your hobby into your profession, but lost your creativity as soon as you were judged by your clients?

The fact that a reward can lower intrinsic motivation poses many problems in reality. After all, we all get paid for our work. Moreover, it sometimes happens that a bonus is paid to one particular employee one year and to someone else the next year. Or worse: that no one receives any awards. Do all kinds of extras have to be withdrawn? Would this mean we can never motivate others extrinsically? Not necessarily, says SDT, because there are different types of extrinsic motivation.

"If people are good only because they fear punishment, and hope for reward, then we are a sorry lot indeed."

ALBERT EINSTEIN

2.2.3   Not every form of extrinsic motivation is the same

By further elucidating the dilemma between intrinsic and extrinsic motivation, Deci and Ryan discovered that there are different types of extrinsic motivation. With each of them having different implications. Specifically, SDT says that there are three[1] types of extrinsic motivation.

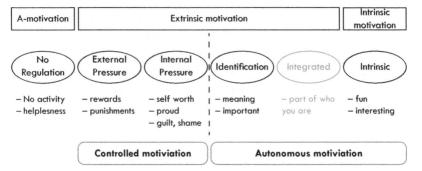

¹ Initially, SDT indicated that there are four types of extrinsic motivation: in addition to "identification" or "meaningfulness" there is also "integration" or "being part of who you are". This motivation occurs for example when nurses care for patients because it is "part of who they are and what they want to do", or when photographers crave for "being creative". But this form of motivation is difficult to distinguish from "meaningfulness" and "intrinsic motivation" in questionnaire research and will therefore be mentioned in the same context as meaningfulness here.

A) *External pressure: when others force you*

The first type of extrinsic motivation is "external motivation" or "external pressure". You let your behavior depend on the judgment of others. This means you work because you have to for others, to meet their expectations, get a reward or avoid punishment. Employees who are externally motivated do their best to obtain job security, get the promotion, receive a bonus, or get more appreciation or less criticism from their boss or family. Their actions depend entirely on others. They only do what they "should" do from others' point of view. So this is a very controlling form of motivation.

CASE

Jerome chose to become a teacher. The many vacations and job security appeal to him. After he graduated, Jerome starts as an interim teacher in different schools at the same time. It is exhausting to constantly get to know new colleagues and computer systems and he soon is fed up with only being able to teach a particular group of students for a short period of

---

time. He can not be happier when he is offered a position in one school for an entire school year. He eagerly looks forward to the permanent position he likely will be offered in this school when he will have been working successfully there a few years in a row. He is very motivated and puts in every effort. He does not like the fact that management regularly asks for his lesson plan and that the inspection audits his teaching materials every few years. But then it finally happens: after a few years he is appointed permanently. Once he reaches his long longed-for goal, his motivation for the work does not improve — to the contrary! The effort and creativity he originally put into his lessons has vanished. He starts to dream of a promotion to become director, but when his application for the position is unsuccessful, his motivation hits rock bottom.

WHAT ABOUT YOU?

To what extent do you work from external pressure?

- Do you work mainly for the money?
- Do you make that extra effort because you hope to be rewarded?
- Do you keep an eye on your emails all evening because your boss expects it?

"Coercion can only end in chaos."

MAHATMA GANDHI

B) *Introjection: when the pressure comes from within yourself*
The second type of extrinsic motivation is "introjection" or "internal pressure". Typical of this form of motivation is that, like external pressure, it is very controlling, but it operates in a more subtle way.

In the case of internal pressure, employees put their self-worth on the line. They feel their self-esteem, ego, status, and recognition are linked to their performance. They are motivated to do a good job so that they do not have to feel afraid, guilty, or ashamed.

Doing a good job in order to "be proud of yourself" can also be linked to introjection. If you take on a job to prove yourself or to be able to boast about the prestigious title, then you are acting from "internal pressure". This is called "hubristic pride": your self-worth is at stake. If you cannot bring something successful or reach the level you had hoped for, then you feel bad and have thoughts like, "I am not worth anything" and "I am a failure". This stands in strong contrast with "authentic pride". This type of pride arises when you have done a meaningful or fun task well and you are proud of your achievement afterwards. In this case, your self-worth is not at stake. You can laugh away at a possible failure with thoughts like, "I will do better next time".

In the case of "internal pressure", the approval or disapproval is no longer sought from external sources such as supervisors, colleagues or family. No, these external influences are to some extent internalized: even in the absence of others, employees feel a certain amount of pressure as they impose this type of pressure on themselves. The "must" comes from within. This can quickly become automatic when managers, colleagues, friends or family members impose things or set high expectations or when employees compare themselves to others.

Many employees are plagued by feelings of guilt and shame. Some are more sensitive to this than others.

CASE

Mia is working in the recruitment and selection department. She loves her job, even though it often becomes too much for her. Her partner and children confront her more and more with the fact that she works long hours. She often schedules interviews in the evening or has to go over emails. "I can't help it," she says, "because these

---

candidates can only free themselves up in the evenings. And during the day, I don't have time for emails." Mia also notices that she is slowly becoming cynical. Her energy level is dropping, she is sleeping less well, and is often short-tempered with her children. One evening her husband asks why she is working so hard. Does she enjoy it? "No," she says. "I would rather do other things, like cooking or exercising". Does she have to work for her boss so much? No, her boss doesn't expect her to put in so many hours. So why does she do it? After some self-reflection, Mia says: "I work so hard because otherwise I would feel guilty." But at the same time, she also feels increasingly guilty toward her husband and children.

WHAT ABOUT YOU?

To what extent do you work from internal compulsions?
— Do you often feel guilty? When you miss a deadline? When you arrive late at work?
— Do you feel ashamed when you close your laptop at 4 p.m. on a Friday, or when, on a day off, you don't check your emails? Or even when you take a day off?
— Do you sometimes work through the evening out of fear of losing your job?

C) *Identification: motivated by meaningfulness*
The third type of extrinsic motivation is called "identification" or "meaningfulness". When meaningfulness is the main motivation, employees are committed to their job because they find their tasks valuable, meaningful or important. Construction workers who identify with their work describe it as "building a home for their customers". And nurses who "help" and "care for" see this as a fundamental part of who they are.

As with external and internal pressure, meaningfulness is a form of extrinsic motivation. Finding something "important" to go for does not always equate to "liking" that activity. Finishing off a house in all weathers is not always fun. And a nurse does not have to find changing her patients' diapers "pleasant" or "enjoyable". But if you identify yourself with your work, then you will also do the tasks that are not fun or pleasant without too many problems, precisely because you recognize their importance or added value.

"Humans are inherently motivated to grow and achieve and will fully commit to and engage in even uninteresting tasks when their meaning and value is understood."

EDWARD DECI & RICHARD RYAN

With the focus on meaningfulness, we have arrived at the core of SDT. SDT is all about meaningfulness and meaning. Here we also say goodbye to the classic assumption that "work should always be fun".
Your work does not always have to be interesting or enjoyable. There are always things that we don't like to do or find less interesting, but if we consider them important and meaningful, then we will carry them out in a high-quality manner.

CASE

— Hans is a researcher who loves to conduct experiments, but he finds it less enjoyable to apply for grants. Still, without grants he can no longer do his job. When Hans realized how important these applications are for the continuation of his job, his motivation improved significantly.

— As an independent consultant, Herman enjoys giving training sessions every day, but his job also involves a lot of administration. Even though he finds this very unpleasant and not interesting, he still spends half a day every week keeping his administration in order. It is a tedious but important part of his job and a "necessary evil" to continue to exist as an independent consultant.

— Marie, an IT worker in a large company, realizes that in addition to optimizing existing tools, the weekly meetings are an important part of her job. She prefers to stay in the background and focus on the numbers and series that she is supposed to monitor. But within the IT team, it is also important to have regular updates on activities. Realizing this enables Marie to perk herself up for meetings and as such she is ready to go every week.

The importance of "meaningfulness" and "meaningful work" is widely recognized within academic literature. We come back to this in the chapters on motivating jobs (Part 2, Chapter 3) and leadership (Part 2, Chapter 5). David Graeber also wrote about it in his book *Bullshit Jobs: A Theory*. Employees who think their jobs don't actually matter experience little meaningfulness in their work. Do you have to spend days writing reports that nobody reads? Will your job be scrapped once you retire or get fired? Or, on the other hand, do you have a job that is valuable to society? As an ambulance driver, you save lives. Or as a cleaner, do you ensure that the toilets remain clean such that people don't get sick.

We don't want to do our work just "for the sake of it", but also because it "makes sense". In a meaningful job, you feel that what you do corresponds with who you are and what you stand for. You have the feeling that your work has impact and contributes to the goal of the organization and is even important for a lot of people outside the organization. You also see that the organization is striving for results in line with your own values (see also the chapter on individual differences, Part 2, Chapter 1).

It can be a liberating thought that, as a business leader or executive, you don't have to make sure that people are always having fun in their work. Your organization should not become an amusement park with pool tables and places to take a nap. Employees are allowed to have fun, absolutely, as enjoying what you do is a powerful type of motivation, but people don't need to enjoy every moment of the day and every task of their job. After all, there are two kinds of happiness: hedonism and eudaimonia.

- *Hedonism* stands for experiencing pleasure, enjoyment and comfort. Hedonists want to feel "good" here and now. It's great and comfortable to eat ice-cream and binge a Netflix series. We know this momentary pleasure and we all aspire to it from time to time.

- *Eudaimonia,* on the other hand, is about whether your life is good. A "good life" means realizing your human potential, with all your talents and shortcomings as best you can to develop yourself and do good for others. Learning a new skill or taking care of others can contribute to such a good life. This is not always fun and can sometimes be very hard. It requires perseverance and often a lot of negative feelings come along with it: we are frustrated when something new doesn't go smoothly, we get angry at a colleague when a project is handled incorrectly and sometimes we find it boring to follow an online training. Yet each of these experiences helps us to continue learning and to grow. And then we become truly happy. The ancient Greeks believed that eudaimonia was the highest good.

"A life full of happiness is important, but it is even much more important to go for a meaningful life."

LEO BORMANS

So as a manager, you don't have to shy away from unpleasant things. It is important to accept what is not pleasant and, above all, to indicate why such matters are nevertheless meaningful and significant. In doing so, try to connect with the perception of the employee. Often a task is valuable to the organization, but the employee does not see its value of for her- or himself. Keeping track of all supporting documentation for a purchase is essential for an audit, but for an individual employee, it can seem like a bullying measure.

WHAT ABOUT YOU?

To what extent do you find your job meaningful?

- How do you make a difference to others in your work?
- Do you indicate why a tedious task is important after all if you delegate it?
- Which tasks have little added value? Can you automate or outsource them?

D) Intrinsic motivation

In addition to the above forms of extrinsic motivation, SDT still places great importance on "intrinsic motivation". This motivation refers to activities for which the motivation lies in the task itself. If you are intrinsically motivated, the reward for the behavior is the behavior itself (so to speak) because you find the activity itself fun or interesting. You find pleasure in writing code as an engineer, in designing buildings as a technical draftsman, or in making electrical circuits perfectly in order as an electrician.

Intrinsic motivation is also seen when people speak passionately about their hobbies or when children become enthusiastically involved in their play. Intrinsic motivation manifests itself in behaviors such as play, exploration, and challenge seeking: all that people do regardless of the prospect of a reward.

CASE

Anne is intrinsically motivated for her work as an accountant. She loves to list numbers in neat Excel sheets and to making sure all her calculations are correct. She sees it as a challenging puzzle that has to be put together from all sides. As a child, Anne already had a preference for order. She sorted her pencils by color and her blocks always fitted neatly in the closet.

WHAT ABOUT YOU?

To what extent are you intrinsically motivated for your work?

— What tasks do you enjoy most?
— What would you do if you won the lottery? Would you still do similar things as you do now at work? Which tasks would you do more and which one's less?

2.2.4 Characteristics of the four motivations

A) *Having to versus wanting to – controlled (low quality) versus autonomous (high quality) motivation*
External pressure, internal pressure and meaningfulness are all forms of extrinsic motivation and thus differ from intrinsic motivation. But they are also very different from each other:

— Employees who start working from external or internal pressure feel pressured, either by others or by themselves. Therefore, these types of motivation are "*controlled*" and of a lower quality. They are accompanied by the feeling: "I must work".

Experienced meaningfulness is of an entirely different order. Employees who find meaning in their work have the feeling that they are in control, they have it "in their own hands". They are no longer pawns moved around the chessboard of life by others. They have the feeling that they control themselves. As with intrinsic motivation, the motivation comes from within and is characterized by the feeling, "I want to" work. Therefore, we consider experienced meaningfulness and intrinsic motivation as "*autonomous motivation*" and High Quality forms of motivation.

B) *Perceived meaningfulness is not intrinsic motivation*
Experienced meaningfulness does differ markedly from intrinsic motivation, because perceived meaningfulness is still extrinsic.

- For example, many employees don't like to clean up their desks after a long working day. It's not a pleasant job. But it does make sense if you want the cleaning team to do their job thoroughly so that you can start your next working day at a clean desk.
- Backing up your computer is usually not great fun; sometimes it is hopelessly complicated and takes up a lot of time. But anyone who has ever lost a lot of data or documents due to a computer crash or stolen laptop will faithfully back up. Not because they expect a compliment from the IT department, but because they think it's important to have that backup in times of need.

In short, intrinsic motivation focuses on pleasure and interest, while with meaningfulness, as the word says, the focus is on the meaning or added value of the task itself.

C) *You can motivate meaningfully extrinsically!*
With the distinction between the different types of extrinsic motivation and the similarity between perceived meaningfulness and intrinsic motivation, we touch on one of the most important assets of SDT. Whereas in the past it was claimed that you had to be "intrinsically" motivated to be "well" motivated, SDT goes further.

SDT shows that being (extrinsically) motivated on the basis of meaningfulness is just as good as intrinsic motivation. Employees who identify with their work typically feel good about themselves, experience little stress and perform well, as do employees who are intrinsically motivated.

Thus, extrinsic motivation is not necessarily problematic. When we are extrinsically motivated for our work but find the work meaningful and/or valuable, we are "well" or "autonomously" motivated.

"Striving for happiness as a life purpose is a mistake. Striving for meaning and significance, on the other hand, is what life is all about."

DIRK DE WACHTER

Extrinsic motivation does tend to be less positive when it involves external or internal pressure. Because then employees have the feeling that they "have to" work and feel controlled. These forms of motivation can be effective, but are often only so in the short term or if you don't expect too much real effort. They are also accompanied by fewer positive and even more negative consequences for the employees' well-being.

Based on SDT, we can say that the distinction between extrinsic and intrinsic motivation is not that important. The difference between controlled and autonomous motivation, or between low- and high-quality motivation makes much more sense for understanding "how well" someone is motivated.

D) *How can you motivate someone for a tedious or unpleasant task?*
Sometimes a task, regulation, or change is imposed without you being able to change it: new software, being obliged to work from home during a pandemic, being part of a self-managing teams, administrative tasks, etc.

Does this mean that you have to control others to do these tasks anyway? Not necessarily. If you impose something on yourself or on someone else, then the question is how the other people deal with it.

- Do they find it fun or interesting? Good, then they are intrinsically motivated, which is a high-quality type of motivation.
- Do they not necessarily find it fun or interesting, but useful? Can they think of a reason why it is valuable? Then this person perceives usefulness in complying with these issues. Great!
- But if they cannot internalize what is imposed, then only controlled motivation or even amotivation remains. So what can you do as a supervisor, coach or colleague? Try to make the task, measure or change fun or, if that fails, explain the meaning of it.

The idea is thus to get someone to move on from possible amotivation, over external and internal pressure, to meaningfulness and enjoyment. The more people shift to the right through these types of motivation, the more their motivation comes from within, and the more they will experience that they themselves shape their own behavior. Such movement is not always easy, but in Part 2 of this book we provide tools that can help you with this.

"If you want to build a ship, don't drum up people to collect wood and don't assign them tasks and work, but rather teach them to long for the endless immensity of the sea."

ANTOINE DE SAINT-EXUPÉRY

CASE

William works as a lab technician in a medical center and has to report weekly on his analyses. William does not really understand why he has to report each week, even though this is very important for invoicing. Isn't the name of the company already mentioned on each sample? So why does he have to invest his (overly busy) time to report on it again? Reporting every week is a heavy burden. William brings his motivation problem to a training session inspired by SDT. "How can he motivate himself to record his time correctly?"

His colleagues soon inspired him. The task remains equally tedious and uninteresting. But thanks to the session, William discovers that Eddy, his colleague in accounting, benefits greatly if he records his time correctly and on time. Eddy never dared to say so, but he needs to deal with a lot of registrations every day, and often he too can no longer see the woods for the trees. William realizes how useful it is that he invests just a bit of time in the reporting. Not for the administration, but for his colleague Eddy.

But the opposite movement can also occur. Instead of going from left to right, you can go from right to left. Someone who is initially autonomously motivated is slowly but surely only going to perform the task because there is a reward attached to it. Needless to say, it is best to avoid this reverse movement.

WHAT ABOUT YOU?

What type of motivation do you hold?

- Are you actually not that motivated for your work?
- Do you do your job mainly under external or internal pressure?
- Do you find your job highly meaningful, fun or exciting?
- Do you combine different kinds of motivations for work?
- Is your motivation different for some tasks than for others? Or does this vary from day to day?

What about you as a supervisor?

- In what ways are your colleagues and team members motivated?
- Can you recall an event in which you had little desire or motivation to act? A task that you even thought was useless, but that you carried out anyway? What gave you the necessary motivation to persevere?
- Can you think of a situation where others put pressure on you?

SUMMARY
People may be motivated for their job for different reasons:

- Andrew just rolled into the job of fishmonger. He helped out in his parents' business and never asked himself whether he liked this job or whether there were other jobs he would rather do. Andrew has amotivation.
- Louise chose the job as a consultant because it pays well. A company car and chance of promotion seemed more important to her than the content of the work. Louise chose this job out of external pressure.
- Paul was bad at chemistry and physics at school. In the meantime he works as a doctoral student in chemistry. He wants to prove himself to his teachers, who had urged him not to choose science. Paul is motivated by internal compulsion or introjection.
- Dora works as a care teacher in elementary school. Helping children with extra exercises is important and valuable for her. Dora is an example of meaningfulness or identification.
- Tom loves his job as a truck driver. He can spend hours on the open road. Tom is intrinsically motivated for his work.

Andrew, Louise, and Paul do their work out of external or internal pessure: an "I have to" motivation. In each case, this involves controlled motivation. Dora and Tom work from experienced meaningfulness or intrinsic motivation, from "I want to" motivation. They are much "better" motivated.

2.2.5 Different motivations, different consequences

The way in which you are motivated has an impact. Different types of motivation each have their own consequences, as was recently summarized in meta-analytic research. In this research more than 100 SDT studies on the impact of the different motivations in the workplace were examined. A meta-analysis summarizes all research conducted to date and thus examines the average effect found in academic literature. It therefore provides highly reliable, substantiated, robust and valid results.

The results show that the different types of motivation largely predict the well-being and performance of employees: up to 40% of the variation in how employees feel and 25 to 30% of the differences in performance can be predicted by the types of motivation. The reported outcomes include, for example:

–   engagement, commitment, or enthusiasm for work:
    the degree in which you have energy, are dedicated
    to your job and can completely immerse yourself in it;
–   job satisfaction;
–   in-role performance: doing what is expected of you;
–   extra role behavior: doing something extra, such as
    replacing a sick colleague or solving a problem even
    before it arises.

This in turn has a positive impact on business performance.

Employees who are autonomously motivated:

— have less stress and a lower risk of burnout;
— are more satisfied and enthusiastic about their work;
— are more involved in their organization: they see the organization as a pleasant place to work and have a warm relationship with it;
— have no intention of leaving;
— perform their duties better;
— solve problems before they arise;
— do something extra now and then: they are more inclined than others to send a card to a sick colleague, help others or volunteer to take on additional projects;
— engage in less negative behavior: they don't bully, loaf less at work and keep far away from sabotage or theft;
— are less absent.

Of all the types of motivation, intrinsic motivation is the strongest predictor: nearly half of the effect of motivation on these outcomes is determined by intrinsic motivation. This is also the only type of motivation that can explain employee absenteeism: Although absence is often and primarily determined by illness, employees who are intrinsically motivated are less likely to be absent than those who find their work less fun or engaging.

Case

Victoria works as a marketing assistant for a well-known fashion designer. She loves the style and designs of her boss, a top designer, and she loves her job. Even when she is diagnosed with breast cancer and her doctor prescribes her two months of rest, there is something that drives her to work. She gets energy from her job, while at home she become depressed. She explains this to her doctor, who also sees that it is better for Victoria to go to work than to doze off on the sofa at home. Of course she is given

---

the freedom to go and rest earlier if she really can no longer manage. Sometimes she is overcome by fatigue and nausea. But for Victoria one thing is clear: because of her work she is better able to deal with the negative effects of her treatment.

"The quality of workers' motivation is predictive not only of their commitment and work effort, but also their overall engagement, well-being and performance in their job."

EDWARD DECI & RICHARD RYAN

Perceived meaningfulness is the second most important motivation. This form of motivation is even more important than intrinsic motivation when it comes to employee performance. Further research is needed to understand this better, but it is speculated that perceived meaningfulness in particular helps to deliver quality work and persevere when the going gets tough.

Remember that last deadline you had to meet? Going the extra mile in the evening or working late into the night to get everything done is not really intrinsically motivating. At times like that, you'd prefer to call it quits and go to bed. But it is the experienced meaningfulness that ensures you still produce high-quality work.

As soon as employees can identify with the meaning and importance of their job, this will increase the quality of their motivation, their well-being and performance.

CASE

Steffi works as an internist in the emergency department of an academic hospital. No matter how hard she has to work, and how difficult it sometimes is to combine work with raising three-year-old twins at home, she finds her job very meaningful and is highly motivated. Even that one time when she has to leave her cute twins' birthday party abruptly. There has been a serious accident and three mortally wounded patients had been taken to hospital by ambulance. She does not like to leave, but at times like this it is the experienced meaningfulness that causes her to say a caring "See you later" to her family and devote herself fully and guilt-free to her patients.

"My contention is that we are too much in a kind of fun culture where everything always has to be fun, cheerful and pleasurable. Social media also promotes this image."

DIRK DE WACHTER

In line with the meta-analytic research on the four types of motivation, studies that focus on autonomous and controlled motivation also point out the value of high-quality motivation. In a study involving more than 500 college teachers, for example, it was found that autonomous motivation led to less burnout.

Research among business school alumni found that autonomous work motivation was associated with greater job satisfaction and less emotional exhaustion. Job satisfaction in turn was related to lower employee turnover, while emotional exhaustion was only correlated with higher employee turnover.

Autonomous motivation also helps to cope well with high work demands: autonomously motivated employees experience less stress with high job demands.

Being motivated from external or internal pressure contributes less to employee well-being and performance. In short, it is detrimental.

Controlled motivation is associated with:

— More stress
— More burnout
— Less engagement

- Less organizational commitment
- More turnover
- Less work effort
- Lower performance

Internal pressure has two faces. On the one hand, internal pressure increases enthusiasm for work, while on the other hand, it also increases stress and longer-term damage. Internal pressure has very little impact on work performance.

External pressure is even worse: although employees will be able to perform under pressure, it is detrimental to their well-being and thus to the long-term success of the organization.

SUMMARY

- Autonomous, "I want" motivation is associated with good results, both for the employees and the organization: a reduced risk of stress and burnout, increased engagement and commitment, reduced turnover, increased work effort, and improved performance. Employees find their work enjoyable, interesting or valuable.
- Controlled, "I have to" motivation usually shows opposite results. Because employees then do their work as a result of internal or external pressure.

2.2.6 Various motivations at the same time: motivation profiles

Above, we discussed motivation from an "either-or" perspective. But reality is more complex than that. Perhaps you also work for different reasons and put effort in your job from multiple motivations: you're happy to get a paycheck every month, you work just a little harder to feel less guilty and at the same time you find your work meaningful and fun. However, the relative weight of each of the four motivations varies from person to person.

In the simplest form of such profile analyses, we distinguish four types of employees:

- The "autonomously motivated" or "wanters" do their work because they "want to": they find their job meaningful, and they are happy to do it. They score high on autonomous motivation and low on controlled motivation.
- The "control-motivated" or "must-doers" do their work because they "have to" or must do it. They work because they are expected to by others (external pressure) or by themselves (internal compulsion). They score high on controlled motivation and low on autonomous motivation.
- The "highly motivated" do their work because they simultaneously have to and want to. They score high on both autonomous and controlled motivation.
- The "unmotivated" are actually not motivated for their work. They score low on both autonomous and controlled motivation.

WHAT ABOUT YOU?

Where do you see yourself in this matrix? Are you a "wanter", a "must doer", a "highly motivated" or an "unmotivated" worker?

And you as a manager?

- Which employees do you prefer to have on your team?
  - Do you prefer wanters – those who only work from a high-quality motivation?
  - Or do you think: "No, give me a group of highly motivated people. All these types of motivations can do no harm. On the contrary, it only makes their motivation stronger."
  - Or do you find autonomous motivation not so important? "Hey, it's fine if they only come to work because they have to. If they are subject to external and internal pressure you can engage

them better with rewards and punishments. If you give them a nice raise, their motivation will also immediately rise. Handy, right?"
- Or does motivation not matter at all? Your employees work, and whether they are strongly, autonomously or control-motivated, or not at all, makes no difference. Motivation is subjective. What matters is their behavior.

When we ask managers which type of employees they prefer, time and again we find that the majority opts for the strongly motivated: "The more motivation, the better". A select few go for the "wanters". Fewer even opt for "must doers". Everyone wants motivated employees on their team, and apparently most feel somewhere that external and internal pressure are not the best ways to motivate employees.

But does the best-performing team consist primarily of highly motivated people?

Both the "wanters" and "highly motivated" have a low risk of burnout and are equally enthusiastic and satisfied about their work. The " must doers ", on the other hand, experience their work as exhausting, have little enthusiasm and derive little satisfaction from it, just like the unmotivated (we have academic references to support these ideas).

A study by HR company Securex, for example, indicates that only 7% of the "wanters" have a risk of burnout. Among the "must doer", this proportion rises to almost half (49%). The "wanters" also distinguish themselves in many other areas: they have a better work capacity, better lifestyle, more energy and enjoy better health. They are also more satisfied with their jobs and their lives.

The distinction between the four groups is also relevant for organizations:

Grant and colleagues, for example, showed that personal initiative only has an impact for those who "want" to work, and thus score high on autonomous and low on controlled motivation. They score better on objective performance indicators, such as the number of job offers and earnings for call center workers.

"Must doers" experience the most stress and tension symptoms and also show twice as much long-term absenteeism. "Wanters" have less stress and are less frequently absent and for less time. They are also more engaged in their work and their organization, are more willing to change, are more innovative and report better performance, less indecision and less procrastination.

These motivational profiles are also important to the society. Securex's data show that autonomously motivated employees, the "wanters", want to work four years longer than the "must doers" and the "unmotivated", and one year longer than the strongly motivated. The "wanters" and "strongly motivated" also say they "can" work two years longer. So there is a long way to go before we are all willing and able to work until retirement age, but for the autonomously motivated workers we are already on the right track.

SUMMARY

Which employees would you prefer to have on your team?

Autonomous motivation is the "best" motivation. Increasing controlled motivation makes little sense or even has a negative effect.

— Wanters have the most ideal motivation profile. For them you just need to create the right environment so that they remain autonomously motivated and do not develop controlled motivation.
— Highly motivated people already have the good, autonomous form of motivation, but combine it with controlled motivation.

Here you can take away some of the control elements so that they can evolve to having only autonomous motivation.

- The trick is to move the unmotivated to more autonomous motivation. Although the stick and carrot can be tempting to get this group going, it comes with a high cost. Sometimes that cost is even higher than if they would remain unmotivated.
- The must doers are the most challenging group. They generally score poorly in terms of well-being and performance. The best thing you can do? Not directly reduce controlled motivation, but increase their autonomous motivation. In a second phase you then bring them from being highly motivated to autonomously motivated.

2.2.7 Motivation for the job or for a particular task?

Just as our motivation for our job cannot be captured in one type, we are also not motivated in the same way for all our tasks. Teachers who are intrinsically motivated to teach, for example, are not necessarily intrinsically motivated to prepare those lessons or – even worse – to keep their administration in order.

Autonomous motivation seems to be reserved for the core tasks of a job, such as teaching by teachers, welding by welders, selling by salespeople, software development for IT professionals, and setting up experiments for researchers. Being autonomously motivated for the core tasks of your job appears to be the most important predictor for job satisfaction and burnout.

Autonomous motivation is also very specific. In your job you can be autonomously motivated for some tasks and not for others. A fashion designer loves designing clothes, but doesn't like organizing fashion shows. Controlled motivation, however, seems to be an oil slick that spreads to all tasks. Some principals keep track of their administration, support their teachers, and take care of the communication in their school all by feeling externally or internally coerced. As soon as you "have" to do one task, chances are this feeling will spread to other tasks. It is therefore important to have a sufficient number of autonomously motivating tasks in your work package in order to keep that oil slick as small as possible.

Whether or not you are autonomously motivated for a task has far-reaching consequences. Employees who are generally well motivated for their work may say they will do certain tasks (e.g., being on time, writing a report), but still they cannot bring themselves to effectively do a good job because they are not properly motivated for that particular task. They may end up not doing the task at all or doing a very poor job.

For example,

–   Only students who indicated that they were autonomously motivated to attend a training course also effectively enrolled. Those who felt compelled to participate let the effective enrollment date pass by.
–   Those who are autonomously motivated to share knowledge and tell colleagues how best to do their job share more and more useful knowledge. Those who feel externally or internally compelled to do so, share less often. Even more: the latter group more often deliberately withholds certain information and pretends not to know when colleagues ask for advice. They say they will help others, but don't do so in reality, or indicate that they cannot simply share their valuable knowledge.

CASE

Jeff, a project manager for a medium-sized construction company, observes during site visits that not all construction workers were wearing their safety helmets. He doesn't understand that. "We provide those helmets for their own safety, why aren't they

---

wearing them?" The site manager indicated that "a safety helmet is annoying and uncomfortable during work." He even provides his construction workers with new helmets because some of them complain about sweat from the previous model. But the new helmets don't help. So, together with the safety coordinator, Jeff set up a toolbox meeting about the safety helmets. They have the construction workers brainstorm together about the arguments for and against wearing a helmet, and then weigh them against each other, two by two, in a fictitious balance sheet. The safety argument emerges as winner: however uncomfortable, the fact that it can save lives proves an important argument for wearing one. Discussing this together increases the autonomous motivation for wearing the helmet. The list of arguments now hangs in every site van.

WHAT ABOUT YOU?

— Do you enjoy doing all your tasks at work?
— Are there things you find less meaningful?
— Do you sometimes promise to do something but do not deliver?
— Do you experience more pressure or stress on some projects than others?

SUMMARY

— If you want people to perform optimally, to feel good and to really engage, it is best to focus on their autonomous motivation.
— Putting employees under pressure to do certain things ensures that they look for ways to get out of it. Or it has even more negative consequences.

The important questions that then arise here are:

- How can you increase the right type of motivation?
- How can you decrease the less efficient types?
- And this for as many tasks as possible.

In other words, how can we increase autonomous motivation, and decrease controlled motivation? You'll read about that in the following chapters.

3. THE BASIC NEEDS: THE ABC OF MOTIVATION

3.1 What are basic needs?

SDT starts from, as McGregor has put it, a Theory Y perspective. Therefore, one of the basic assumptions is that people – including employees, executives, managers and colleagues – are naturally growth-oriented and want to develop. But this growth-oriented nature of people does not automatically emerge. It takes good support to do so. According to Deci and Ryan, the founders of SDT, such support needs to take the form of the satisfaction of our basic psychological needs. Satisfaction of these needs is the fundamental nutrient we need to feel psychologically good.

So far, three needs have been identified as crucial. To identify these needs, you can do the following exercise:

Close your eyes for a moment and think of a moment when you felt really good, when you were bursting with energy and were completely yourself.
What moment are you thinking of? What characterizes this moment?

Time and again this assignment brings up the three basic psychological needs that SDT also considers crucial. They form its ABC.

- A stands for Autonomy.
- B stands for Belongingness.
- C stands for Competence.

"SDT considers autonomy, competence and relatedness to be essential ingredients for sustained motivation and nutrients for individual growth, well-being and thriving."

EDWARD DECI & RICHARD RYAN

Just as we need food, water and a roof over our heads to feel physically good, according to SDT we need the satisfaction of these three psychological basic needs to feel psychologically good. We need it in order to be happy, to be positive in life, and to give the best of ourselves. For the work context, this means all your employees are better (though not necessarily more) motivated, feel better at work, and perform better as soon as their ABC is fulfilled. Even when they are not aware that they have these needs.

In the rest of the book we refer to the satisfaction of the three basic needs for autonomy, belongingness, and competence as "the ABC".

CASE

Frank, a truck driver, is one year from retirement. He tells his supervisor that he wants to retire early. "Very regrettable," the supervisor responds, "but would you be willing to fill in during the vacation period? After all, you were such a good driver, you never caused an accident, you have not made many mistakes, and you were an example for the others!" The result of this conversation is that Frank continues to work until his retirement. Why? At the time of the announcement of his departure, he had received, for the first time in his career, positive feedback — or just plain feedback from his supervisor. For the first time he felt "that his work mattered" and that he was valued.

WHAT ABOUT YOU?

To what extent...

- do you feel free to make choices at work?
- do the decisions you make in your job reflect what you really want?
- do you have a good relationship with other people at work?
- can you successfully complete difficult assignments at work?
- are you able to finish your work well?

3.2 The ABC of motivation

3.2.1 Autonomy

The need for autonomy is perhaps the most particular need within SDT. This is because SDT defines autonomy differently than many other (motivation) theories. In the work context, being able to work "autonomously" is often seen as a situation in which employees can decide everything themselves: they can or must decide which tasks to take on and how, where and when to work. It seems to be about "me, me, me".

But within SDT, autonomy takes on a different meaning. It is not about being able to decide everything *yourself*, but being able to stand behind your actions. If your car is going in the direction you want it to go, being in the passenger seat is sometimes just as nice as being in the driver's seat. You don't always have to be in control of the car, as long as it is going in a direction you value. So, with SDT, it's about being *"psychologically free"*, feeling you are able to do the things that are in line with who you are, and not do things "against your will". At work you may not be able to decide which projects, customers or patients will come your way, but maybe they appeal to you in such a way that you experience the autonomy to go to work on them volitionally.

When your need for autonomy is not met, or even frustrated, you feel like you are being forced to do things you don't want to do. You are not allowed to be yourself and have no control over what happens in your life. In other words, anyone who feels frustrated in their need for autonomy has the feeling of having to do all sorts of things "against their will".

Your need for autonomy at work is fulfilled when you:

- experience being allowed to be yourself;
- experience choice and psychological freedom;
- can express your ideas;
- stands behind your tasks and decisions;
- can give input on how you preferably perform a task;
- initiate your own actions instead of being forced by your boss, colleagues, or even customers.

Your need for autonomy at work is frustrated when you:

- feel like you have a lot of things to do;
- feel compelled to do a lot of things that you wouldn't choose;
- experience that your work is a chain of obligations;
- have the feeling that the situation is taking over from you.

Note that autonomy is not the same as independence. Autonomy does not mean making each decision on your own. Indeed, feeling satisfied in your need for autonomy is unrelated to how dependent you are on others at work. Thus, you can find yourself in four different situations:

Independent of others and autonomous	Dependent on others but autonomous
You can choose what you do and how you do it, without having to rely on others to do so. You also feel that you fully support your own choices. Think of the gardener who can choose for himself whether he first tackles the hedges or first prunes the fruit trees.	You can cooperate in projects that you fully support, even though you've had no choice in the matter and/or you are dependent on others. Take, for example, a prevention advisor who cannot choose which difficulties he is called upon and with whom he must cooperate, but who can offer help and advice voluntarily and autonomously.
Independent of others and non-autonomous	**Dependent on others and non-autonomous**
Here you are independent of others, but still do not feel satisfied in your need for autonomy. For example, you have so many choices that you don't quite know what to choose or where to start. Think of a cleaning lady who works in the home of a family she has never met. A cleaning lady who has to bring the entire house in order all by herself, without instructions, structure or knowing what that family considers important.	Because you are dependent on others, you feel compelled to do things that you would rather not do or do differently. This happens, for example, when employees on the assembly line are completely dependent on how fast or slow the belt goes, and have little or no say in this. Because the belt goes too fast for some operations and too slow for others, they do not feel autonomous.

"Freedom consists in recognizing boundaries."

KRISHNAMURTI

The more autonomy, the better? A frequent pitfall after an initial introduction to the ABC of SDT is that executives remember that they need to give their employees more freedom. If you look at it from an SDT point of view, you cannot give employees too much "psychological freedom", but certainly too much actual "freedom" or "independence". And when you do, there is a good chance that this will turn out negatively. Because when you provide "total freedom" to your employees, you don't create more satisfaction of the basic need for autonomy as described by SDT, but rather the feeling of "being left all by yourself" or even "chaos".

For example, some employees experience too much freedom when working from home and will therefore function less well. They end up in a situation that offers too little structure for them and they do not know what to do. The idea is to focus on the individual and offer just enough structure and guidelines within which your employees can function and act autonomously.

So you don't necessarily meet the need for autonomy by delegating everything or by introducing self-managing teams. Offering structure is crucial. There are still things that need to be done. A comparison with the educational context can help understand this: children may choose whether to use mint or strawberry flavored toothpaste, but they have to brush their teeth.

CASE

Two weeks before a team building event, Tina receives an email from her boss: "As agreed in March, on our next team day you will all receive assertiveness training. Your contribution for this is 180 dollars." Tina feels resistance reading this mail. At the time of the agreement, Tina did not yet work in the team, so she was not aware of it. Does this mean that Tina should drop out of the training in order to satisfy her need for autonomy? Not necessarily. It is just annoying that this has not been communicated when planning the team day a few weeks before. It isn't so much the training that caused resistance, but rather the way in which it all happens. Tina has the feeling that she has no choice, that it is being imposed on her and she is faced with a *fait accompli*. If her boss would tell her more about the training, she can experience more autonomy leading up to the team day.

3.2.2 Belongingness

The need for connection, relatedness or belongingness is satisfied in the workplace when people feel liked and cared for by others, allowed to care for and like other people, and when they experience a stable, balanced bond with colleagues, supervisors and/or customers. Employees feel connected to others at work when they can talk about what is on their mind, when they are helped in difficulties and are also allowed to show their concern for others.

When your need for belongingness is frustrated, you feel that you are not part of a warm group and have no one to turn to. You then have the feeling that people close to you actually don't like you or are even bullying and undermining you. You think that your colleagues and boss cannot be trusted and you feel lonely and isolated.

Your need for belongingness at work is fulfilled when you:

— experience warm, close and authentic bonds with your colleagues, clients, boss and everyone around you;
— genuinely care for others;
— feel loved;
— are part of a group or multiple groups;
— feel a sense of belonging;
— feel accepted by your colleagues;
— can trust your colleagues;
— are trusted by your team members.

Your need for connection at work is frustrated when you:

— feel excluded, ignored, bullied or hurt;
— have no one to turn to;
— feel rejected by your colleagues or supervisor.

Psychology has long emphasized the importance of connection and belongingness. Such a need is for example also central in Maslow's pyramid. Although this theory has never been scientifically validated, it does point to the need for "love and belonging", which is the first psychological need after the more physical needs such as food, drink and security. The American psychologist Harlow also showed with his experiments on monkeys that warm security is essential for survival. The monkeys would rather cling to a soft surrogate mother made of terry cloth than to an iron doll holding a porridge bottle.

CASE

Bill works as an occupational physician. Even though he meets patients all day, he does not feel that he belongs to a close-knit group at work. He hardly ever speaks to his fellow physicians, and often he notices that his patients are not entirely honest with him. He does not experience real connection in his work and therefore doubts whether he would continue his job.

"The things that matter most in our lives are not fantastic or grand. They are moments when we touch one another."

JACK KORNFIELD

The need for belongingness goes beyond classic team building events with exciting exercises around trust or building connections. Such activities are certainly valuable and can be a valuable part of team building, but belongingness really means that you share life's ups and downs on a regular basis and experience the necessary depth and connection.

Helping each other to meet deadlines, being able to ventilate grievances after a bad meeting and ask each other sincerely, "How are you", provide more satisfaction of the need for belongingness. The quality rather than the quantity of relationships is put forward in various studies as the most important predictor of happiness.

> *"We sometimes forget that life is a bit difficult at times. And we have to dare to share that with each other. If we talk about it, we will be connected. It is especially in the sharing of difficulty that we become very, very close to each other."*

DIRK DE WACHTER

CASE

Aline enjoys doing her job, but relations with her colleagues seem to have soured somewhat in recent years. For her, meeting up after work with colleagues is not necessary. Nor does she feel the need to constantly exchange texts with them. Because Aline does not participate enthusiastically outside of work, she feels that she's losing touch with her colleagues at work. She also feels the rest of the team sometimes goes too far. For example, when the manager asked if everyone had arrived on time that morning, the team members did not mention that one of them was routinely late. They covered for each other. There is so much collegiality expected in the group that lies are allowed.

Instead of a close-knit team in which everyone can find his/her place, the team has become a clique with strict rules; and little satisfaction of the need for relatedness.

3.2.3 Competence

People feel satisfied in their need for competence when they feel that they have an *effect on the world* and can achieve what they are committed to. When employees are allowed to do things at work that they are good at and further develop their talents and competencies, they feel competent.

Those who feel frustrated in their need for competence think that they won't be able to achieve their goals, have doubts about everything they do, are insecure, fear failure and often feel they are a disappointment.

Your need for competence at work is fulfilled when you:

- feel competent to perform the task or activity;
- think you can achieve the desired goals;
- can develop your own competence;
- feel successful in your role;
- are good at your job;
- get opportunities to develop your skills;
- master your tasks and experience a sense of mastery;
- can grow, learn, and evolve, even if it is by making mistakes.

Your need for competence at work is frustrated when you:

- are disappointed time and again in your own abilities;
- experience fear of failure;
- doubt that you can do your job;
- think you can't do something (well enough).

---

*"If you can't explain it to a six-year-old,
you don't understand it yourself."*

ALBERT EINSTEIN

CASE

Jonas works as a data manager for the government. He enjoys his job, has a keen eye for efficiency and has already completed several processes and projects across different departments. Because he can unblock things and is averse to any office politics, he is also very popular with his colleagues, even across departments. With Ivan's imminent retirement, management sees in him the ideal candidate to take over Ivan's managerial tasks. But Jonas's supervisor sees things differently. He knows that management is not Jonas's passion and puts Steven forward for the new position. Jonas is more interested in IT processes and data. Steven also has talent for creating order out of chaos, and on top of that he enjoys working with people. And management has no reason to regret having chosen Steven, who turns out to be an excellent manager, while Jonas can continue working on IT projects that gave him lots of energy. Both are deployed in a place where they feel competent.

SUMMARY

OUR BASIC NEEDS

Autonomy	Belongingness	Competence
– Being allowed to be yourself	– Close, warm, authentic bond	– Feeling competent and effective
– Acting, thinking and feeling freely	– Caring for others	– Learning, growing, developing skills
– Choice	– Being loved, being part of a group	– Reaching goals

3.3   Characteristics of the ABC

Seven characteristics typify these three basic needs.

1)   They are psychological
SDT's ABC needs are about our psychological functioning. So they are not about our physical basic needs for food, drink, sleep and sexual contacts. Those are important too, of course. Because it is difficult to work when you are hungry, thirsty or lack sleep, even if your psychological basic psychological needs are fulfilled.

2)   They are essential
Satisfying or fulfilling the ABC radically increases our well-being and stimulates great performance. Frustrating them encourages problematic behavior.

3)   They don't have to be explicit
We don't have to "consciously" experience the needs. Even people who say that they don't necessarily want good relationships at work will flourish once they feel they belong.

4)   They are innate

They are part of our human nature. Even small children feel better when their basic psychological needs are met.

5)   They are universal

Everyone experiences these three needs, and they bring about growth and well-being in everyone. Whether you work as a laborer or clerk, are old or young, introverted or extroverted... We all flourish as soon as we feel that our basic needs are met.

6)   Everyone can fulfill these needs differently

The amount of autonomy you give to one team may be different from the autonomy another team can handle. While for an introvert one good conversation may be enough to feel connected, extroverts are more likely to experience connection at a busy reception. And some feel competent to perform a task as soon as they understand 60% of it, while others only feel competent at a "big award". One thing is certain, no matter how you fill your basic need, when it is fulfilled, you will "function optimally".

7)   Each of these ABC needs is equally important

Unlike in Maslow's reasoning, within SDT one need does not necessarily have to be satisfied before the others are relevant. The three basic needs are strongly linked: whoever feels connected will experience autonomy more easily than those who feel less connected. You also feel more autonomous when you can do things you are good at. But it may happen that one need is satisfied, while the others are not satisfied at all. For example, you may have chosen for a certain project (high autonomy) in a nice project team (high belongingness), but you fear that you do not have the necessary skills or abilities (low competence). SDT predicts that for these projects you will also be less motivated than if all your needs were met.

"Regardless of our many differences, we all have the same needs. What differs is the strategy for fulfilling these needs."

MARSHALL B. ROSENBERG

WHAT ABOUT YOU?

How are your basic needs being met at work?

—   To what extent is your ABC currently fulfilled?
—   What can you do to experience even more ABC?
—   Think of a situation where one or more basic needs are frustrated.
    ·   How can you change these to a situation where they are fulfilled?
    ·   What do you need from yourself for this? And from your colleagues? Your supervisor?

What about the basic needs of your employees?

—   Are they fulfilled?
—   What are you doing to fulfill their ABC?
—   What more could you do?
—   What do you need for this from your environment, your manager, your organization?
—   Can you name a situation in which you, consciously or unconsciously, frustrated someone's needs?
    ·   Which need was on the line?
    ·   How did that happen?
    ·   How did the person react?

3.4 Consequences of fulfilling or not fulfilling the ABC

Is the ABC important? Research in the context of SDT clearly shows that it is. The satisfaction of basic needs is accompanied by a lot of positive consequences, while failure to satisfy or even frustrate the ABC has a negative impact.

Based on meta-analytic studies and reviews that compile the literature, we can conclude that satisfaction of basic needs is associated with:

– *More autonomous motivation*

The ABC helps in the development of autonomous motivation. Those who can commit themselves in all freedom and wholeheartedly to their work, have pleasant colleagues and have the feeling that their efforts have an effect will also experience their work as more and more meaningful or enjoyable and thus become more autonomously motivated for their work.

– *Optimal functioning in the workplace*

Meta-analytic research shows that those who feel fulfilled in their ABC at work function "optimally" in the workplace. That is to say, they feel good about themselves, have a positive outlook and perform the best they can. This means that that person:

– experiences less stress and has a lower risk of burnout;
– is more enthusiastic and satisfied at work;
– is more committed to the organization;
– is happier both in terms of eudaimonic and hedonic well-being;
– has less intention of leaving the organization;
– performs better, is more creative and does more than what is asked;
– is less absent due to illness;
– persists longer, even with difficult tasks;
– exhibits fewer problematic behaviors such as tardiness, taking extra breaks or hiding mistakes;
– uses less alcohol and/or drugs at work.
– A better, healthier and more vital life

The fulfillment of the ABC needs at work also has a broader impact than merely on your work context. Also outside the office walls or work floor employees who see their ABC fulfilled at work feel that they:

- are healthier, both physically and mentally;
- have more energy;
- experience more positive emotions, such as joy and energy;
- experience fewer negative emotions, such as fear, frustration, anger and sadness;
- are less emotionally exhausted;
- are more satisfied with their lives; in short, are happier.

Older employees who find need satisfaction in their work are less prone to take early retirement, and business leaders who find their basic needs met feel more committed to their own company. Also, for employees with long-term illnesses, needs satisfaction has positive effects. When they feel autonomous, belonging, and competent in volunteering on a farm, they are more willing to return to work. Frustration of basic needs, in turn, has opposite effects.

Work stress and negative behaviors such as bullying and aggression especially come to the fore when the ABC is frustrated, meaning that:

- when employees really feel they are being forced to do things they don't support;
- when employees feel lonely and isolated, have a conflict at work or there is little trust;
- when employees have fear of failure, have to do things they cannot do or have no impact on.

Such effects are found not only in Western countries, but also in China and Latin America. (Re)satisfying the ABC helps to reverse these negative effects.

CASE

When we look at the way this book came about, we all felt satisfied in our basic needs. We were fortunate enough to be able to give each other time when writing, so that each time we could sit at our desks on our own initiative and voluntarily. The moments when it went smoothly we were in a flow and felt connected with each other and our publisher. There was a strong trust between us, even when we were each at our own computers. So you don't have to be physically present to feel you belong. Because we have all been involved with SDT on a daily basis for many years, our need for competence is more than fulfilled when we talk and write about it. Especially since we can call on each other and a whole group of other SDT researchers whenever something is unclear. And we can draw on a long list of practical examples. The writing process also brought a lot of new insights. This way all of us kept growing and learning, and our sense of competence increased every day. We experienced the writing process as fun and meaningful.

WHAT ABOUT YOU?

What happens when...

- you can be yourself 100% at work?
- you can work together with great colleagues with whom you are on the same page?
- you meet a tough deadline?
- you are forced to do things you do not agree with?
- the atmosphere among colleagues drops below zero?
- you have to start a task you think you cannot do?

SUMMARY

IMPLICATIONS AND CONSEQUENCES OF ABC NEEDS

Fulfillment of ABC needs	Frustration of ABC needs
— More autonomous motivation	— More controlled motivation
— Less stress	— More stress
— Optimal functioning	— More counterproductive behavior
— Higher well-being	— Lower well-being
— Better, healthier and more vital life	

Since the ABC needs are associated with a lot of positive consequences, it is crucial to understand what can make you and your employees feel more autonomous, belonging, and competent. How to make that happen is covered in Part 2, where we look at practical tools to better motivate people.

PART 2

TOOLS TO START WORKING WITH
SELF-DETERMINATION THEORY

1. PERSONAL DIFFERENCES IN MOTIVATION

WHAT ABOUT YOU?

— Are you quickly enthusiastic for all kinds of tasks?
— Do you easily see the use of what others ask of you?
— Do you feel guilty when you are not at work?
— Do you feel easily controlled?

SDT starts from a number of basic principles that apply to everyone:

— Everyone is born with the inherent desire and possibility to grow and develop.
— Everyone has a need for autonomy, belongingness, and competence (ABC). When these three needs are met, everyone feels good, has a positive outlook on life, and gives their best. Frustration of these needs has the opposite effect.
— Autonomous motivation has a positive impact on everyone, while controlled motivation has a negative impact.

Even though everyone, regardless of their personality, has the same three basic needs, and even though they will increase autonomous motivation for everyone, people may differ in the degree to which they realize and have their basic needs met and/or are more easily controlled than autonomously motivated. This is because our motivation depends on both our environment (as we will discuss later) and our personal characteristics. In this chapter we look at characteristics that differ between people.

— Some of these characteristics are fixed, such as your gender, age, education, culture, and certain personality traits.

- Others may evolve over time. They depend on your previous experiences, your upbringing, training courses you attend, as well as the way you look at your surroundings, how mindful you are, and your personal values.

DO YOU THINK…

- older workers have different needs than younger ones?
- it is best not to give workers too much autonomy?
- only highly educated people can be autonomously motivated?
- low-skilled workers can only be motivated through punishment and reward?
- low-skilled jobs are less meaningful?
- women have a greater need for connection?
- men are more concerned with power and status symbols?

1.1 Demographic characteristics and personality

When we look at a number of fixed personality characteristics, we see little difference between employees in terms of *gender*: men and women are equally likely to fulfill their ABC and experience autonomous motivation.

We also find no differences in terms of *education level*. Higher and lower educated people benefit equally from autonomy, belongingness, and competence. Organizations tend to focus mainly on the ABC of their executives and higher management. Workers and the lower educated are all too often overlooked. They get a lot fewer, or only task-related, training opportunities. But they too will flourish and perform better if their needs for autonomy and connection are more satisfied by their work environment.

What may differ, however, is the way these needs are met. A team of highly educated researchers is given autonomy in a different way than a team of assembly line workers. What is crucial here is that you zoom in on how they want their needs to be met. The case of Peter and his welders (Part 1, Section 1.4) shows convincingly that this works. But there is more.

CASE

A large company in a big international port employs a lot of workers of different nationalities. Loading and unloading, transportation… All these tasks have to be carried out in all weathers. Workers and engineers work side by side and the collaboration goes smoothly despite the differences in nationality and language. They have to work hard, but there is also time for fun and laughter. "Work hard, play hard" is their motto. The jokes fly back and forth and there is mutual respect for each other's jobs and skills. Yet there is also resentment within the group. Everyone works in the open air, and sometimes they feel like a hot cup of coffee or soup. Workers can get one at the vending machine for 90 cents, while engineers can have free coffee, all day long. In this way management wants to reward and appreciate the engineers. But what happens? The engineers feel bad about the situation, and every time they make coffee for themselves, they ask the workers nearby if they would like a coffee as well. Thus they circumvent management's "divide and rule" policy, and strengthen the feeling and sense of solidarity with the workers. The latter appreciate this enormously and in exchange for a simple cup of coffee, more jokes fly across the table. The workers would go through fire for those friendly, respectful engineers.

Research shows that *older* employees and employees with high levels of *seniority* are slightly more likely to feel autonomous and competent. The longer you are in a job, the more autonomy you get and the more experience you have. As a result, older employees may become increasingly autonomously motivated for their work. This contradicts the common notion that employees from a certain age would no longer be motivated for their work.

Of course, some older employees are less motivated. But this also applies to some younger employees and those between the ages of 35 and 45. The former are not always eager for their jobs, while the latter are at the peak of their lives, where both career and family are in development and require attention.

Older employees do tend to be motivated differently for their jobs: for the time they have left in the workplace they are less willing to get involved in new things they do not see the added value of (e.g., a training course on a new skill that they may never need). Thus, they are more likely to look for meaningfulness in their work. In addition, they find good relationships very important. It is therefore unfortunate to note that older employees feel less connected at work.

In terms of *personality*, there are some differences. The basis of our personality can be summarized, according to the academic literature, in five personality traits: openness, conscientiousness, extraversion, agreeableness, and neuroticism. People vary on these from low to high and everything in between.

These characteristics are fairly stable throughout our lives and employees who score high on certain traits (agreeableness, for example) feel their basic needs are met more easily than others.

Those who are friendly and have a warm, cooperative, and committed attitude will more easily feel autonomous, belonging, and competent than those who are less pleasant in social interaction. The same is true for extroverts. They seek out others more easily, because they get energy from social contacts, which are a crucial source for fulfilling our ABC. Also, employees who are careful and/or emotionally stable feel more easily satisfied in their basic needs. There is no correlation between openness and ABC, though.

Does this mean you will always experience little ABC if you are less friendly, extroverted, careful, or emotionally stable? Certainly not! For one thing, personality traits are not an all-or-nothing story, but rather, people differ in degrees. Second, the relation between personality traits and satisfaction of the ABC is minor. Some other personality traits and, of course, social environment plays a much larger role.

One particular "personal trait" that merits more attention is *workaholism*. Workaholics spend a lot of time at and on their work. They work a lot harder than their colleagues and harder than the organization expects them to. If they are not at work, they feel guilty. They are constantly thinking about work, even when they are not working. They work compulsively. Working "has to be done". Thus, workaholics are preoccupied with their work all the time. Yet, they are not happy, but experience a lot of stress and run a high risk of burnout.

For family members, colleagues and the organization, workaholism has many disadvantages. It is assumed that workaholics are highly motivated, which they are. But as we pointed out in Part 1, being highly motivated is not always positive. And this is especially true for workaholics.

Working hard or putting in many hours – the behavioral component of work addiction – can happen for a variety of reasons.

- Do you work hard because you find it fun or meaningful? From an autonomous motivation perspective? If so, this increases your energy level, well-being, and health.
- Do you work hard because you feel obliged to? From a controlled motivation perspective? Then this diminishes your energy level, well-being, and health.

So working hard in itself doesn't hurt, but it becomes problematic when you do it from a sense of compulsion. And that's where the rubber hits the road. Workaholics work compulsively, partly because of their focus on extrinsic rewards, such as a high salary or a nice car. But they are especially obsessive with work from an internal pressure. All of this undermines their well-being and performance. Compulsive working therefore has negative effects on their health.

CASE

Luc knows his stuff. If he receives an urgent question from a customer, he knows very well whom to pass it on to. Tom has never refused. Two weeks ago, for example, he asked Tom on a Friday evening to finish a file by Monday. Luc could see that Tom didn't really want to, but still, Tom immediately called his girlfriend to tell her he couldn't come along on the weekend. His work needed him. That was not the first time he had cancelled a private appointment. He is always the first to arrive at work and the last to leave. He never takes lunch breaks. Even on vacation he takes his work with him. He simply cannot say "No".

What can you do if you have a workaholic on your team? It is important for both managers and the broader organization to identify workaholics. Not by looking at the number of hours employees work: enthusiastic employees can work as many hours as workaholics. But by looking at their motivation. Do they work from autonomous motivation? Do they find their work fun, engaging, and meaningful? Or do they work so hard from internal or external pressure?

Once you know who in your team is addicted to their work, you don't need to take their work away from them. But you can make sure they work less compulsively. This is possible in several ways.

TIPS

Do you have a workaholic on your team?

— Make them aware of their feelings of internal compulsion. Point out that guilt, shame, and fear are poor motivators.

- Provide as little external pressure as possible.
- Reduce their stressors, such as workload, role conflicts, and emotional demands.
- Increase their energy resources, such as social support and their sense of control over their job.

The research on workaholism reaffirms how important it is to be properly motivated for work. Highly motivated employees may either feel very good and function optimally at their work, or they don't feel good and show problematic behaviors. Which direction they go depends on which motivation is driving their behavior. Therefore, it is important to not encourage their controlled motivation, but their autonomous motivation, by focusing on their ABC.

WHAT ABOUT YOU?

- Are you addicted to your work?
- Do you work primarily from internal or external pressures?
- Do you work hard? Harder than your colleagues?
- Do you dare to stop early without feeling guilty?

What about you as a manager?

- Do you think you have workaholics on your team?
- Do you do anything to lower their feelings of pressure?

1.2 Sensitive to pressure?

WHAT ABOUT YOU?

What would you do in the following situations?

A colleague is offered a job you have also applied for. What do you think about this?

a) Actually, you did not expect to get the job, you are often passed over or skipped.
b) Your colleague probably got the job politically by following the rules of office politics.
c) You take a critical look at your performance and find out why your colleague would have been offered the job.

One of your employees is suddenly performing a lot less than normal. What do you do?

a) You tell him that his work no longer meets expectations and that he needs to work harder.
b) You ask him if there is a problem and let him know that you are available to talk about it.
c) You actually have no idea how to help him or what to do.

You can respond to and look at the work situations described above in three ways:

- you respond empathetically and are task-oriented (1C, 2B);
- you react by being controlling and coercive (1B, 2A); or
- you simply resign yourself to this (1B, 2C).

While the first reaction is most likely when you have an autonomous orientation, the second and third are more likely when you have a controlled or an impersonal orientation, respectively.

Employees with an autonomous orientation:	Employees with a controlled orientation:	Employees with an impersonal orientation:
– are attentive to, or seek out, things that satisfy their needs and stimulate their autonomous motivation, such as optimally challenging tasks, an intrinsically motivating job, and reasons why an activity that is not particularly enjoyable in itself may still be important; – experience a great deal of self-determination and choice; – have high self-esteem; – are in control of their own lives; – take responsibility for their behavior; – view social contexts as supportive; – engage because they find something meaningful, fun, or interesting.	– attach more importance to what others demand or expect than what they want for themselves; – look for possible external rewards; – feel obligated to satisfy "important" others and agree to their advice and suggestions; – are concerned about their ego, power, status, and other extrinsic aspects of their work; – view their social environment as controlling; – put pressure on themselves to meet the expectations and standards of others. Thus, they prevent the fulfillment of their ABC and are motivated from internal and external pressure.	– feel unable to influence their environment; – believe that achieving desired results is beyond their control; – attribute their own success to luck or fate; – feel they have no control over the world. No matter how much effort they make, they can never achieve their desired goal; – experience a lack of motivation as a result; – often feel anxious and ineffective.

From our upbringing and previous experiences, each of us develops each orientation to a greater or lesser extent. But we differ in the degree to which we have all three. These orientations are activated by socio-contextual factors: they fluctuate as a function of the people with whom we interact and the context in which we find ourselves.

– Those who are more autonomously oriented see more opportunities to fulfill their ABC and are more autonomously motivated.
– Those who are more control-oriented are more likely to experience pressure from others or themselves. Such people have a harder time fulfilling their ABC and are more often control-motivated.

–   Those who are more likely to be impersonally oriented often feel powerless, hopeless, or desperate and are more often amotivated.

1.3   Mindfulness

Mindfulness is an open attention to and awareness of the present moment. You look intently at what is happening within yourself and your wider environment, without judgment. Not everyone is equally mindful. People who are mindful in life are more aware of the different phenomena that are going on inside them, such as their emotions, impulses, values, and needs. They also have a better view of what is happening around them.

Mindfulness helps you:

1. to become more in touch with, and regulate, your own emotions. It increases your capacity to tolerate unpleasant and stressful emotions by keeping a healthy distance from them. You learn that you "are" not but "have" emotions, and that they come and go. This is also shown in neurological research. By judging your emotions less, you accept them more. This allows you to follow your own interests and values more instead of letting yourself be led by momentary impulses and emotions.
2. to become more aware of your surroundings. This allows you to better recognize the many temptations in and around yourself, and become less susceptible to external and internal pressure. You focus more on values that really matter, such as your health and being there for others. This better awareness subsequently ensures that you make better and more thoughtful choices. "Do I wrap up this sale quickly to brush up my quarterly figures, or do I wait a few more calls so I can really help the customer with what he needs?"

WHAT ABOUT YOU?

- Do you sometimes find it difficult to keep your attention on your work?
- Do you often work on "automatic pilot"?
- Are you often already thinking about what you have to do tomorrow?
- Do you sometimes only half listen while you're busy with other things?

Mindfulness has many benefits:

- More satisfaction of your ABC: If you don't know your own needs or how to satisfy them, it's not easy to fulfill them. Identifying and naming your own needs helps you to come up with your own strategies to satisfy them. You can also share your needs with others. When you express your needs, it becomes easier to see them fulfilled.
- More autonomous motivation: When you are mindful, you work less from external or internal pressure and so you are less motivated by controlled reasons. You place less value on punishments, criticism from others, or financial resources. Social pressure becomes less salient and you need less affirmation from others. Employees who are mindful appeal more to their inner compass and therefore experience more pleasure in their tasks and experience their work as more meaningful.
- Better coping with stressful situations: Mindfulness can buffer for the impact of a negative work climate and helps dealing with work demands. Those who are mindful can better handle pressure from the environment and are less affected by it. Mindful employees evaluate situations as less stressful and regard emotional work demands (e.g., difficult customers, patients who are having a hard time, a tight deadline) as less stressful. A possible explanation is that mindfulness allows you to disconnect your emotions from yourself, making you judge them less. As a result, your own (negative) emotions

come across as less overwhelming or threatening. Of course, mindfulness cannot completely remove the negative effects of a controlling work climate or stressors. Employees will still perform best when their ABC is effectively supported.

"The feeling that any task is a nuisance will soon disappear if it is done in mindfulness."

Thích Nhất Hạnh

– Helping others more and better: Mindfulness ensures that you, in turn, are more open to what others really need. So you become better at satisfying the needs of others. Employees with mindful leaders are therefore lucky. Mindful leaders satisfy their employees' ABC more effectively, which subsequently improves their satisfaction and work performance. Employees of mindful leaders also take on additional tasks such as helping their colleagues and thinking proactively. They also become more mindful themselves. Those who can take care of others and fulfill their ABC become, as a result, happier themselves! Mindfulness thus helps to set a positive spiral in motion, both for yourself and for others.

CASE

Eva suffers from stress quite often. Recently she read about a training in mindfulness. Although at work she was offered such a training before, she had never considered taking part. But now that she could choose to take the training herself, it appealed to her. At the course she learned to take a different perspective, to be without judgments, to become aware of what was going on inside herself, and to become more aware of the situations in which she found herself, more attuned to her own values and needs. She found that her stress disappeared by training her concentration and focus, but it went much further. She became more in touch with her emotions and needs and realized that she was not "being" her emotions and needs. She experienced them but was also able to distance herself from them and observe them without being controlled by them. Although Eva sometimes found it scary to face her own fears, she learned to take more responsibility for her needs and emotions. She no longer ran away from them or tried to push them away with food or drink. It also helped her at work. By no longer being controlled by her emotions, she was better able to deal with the edgy behavior of her colleagues. The fact that Jerome rarely if never wished her good morning bothered her less now. For she now realized better that he liked to concentrate once he was at work. When she was in a good mood, she sometimes brought him a coffee from the vending machine later in the day. Then he often had time for a little break.

WHAT ABOUT YOU?

- Do you sometimes take a break?
- What do you experience now? Are you stressed, quiet, enthusiastic, calm?
- What does your environment look like? Warm, cold, calm? What do you smell?
- What do you hear?
- Which of your needs are currently met? Which are not yet satisfied?

Mindfulness can be trained:

Because research shows that mindfulness has many benefits, the interest in mindfulness has risen sharply in recent years. Studies show that mindfulness can be learned and – once adopted in the workplace – also has many benefits for both employees and organizations. By taking a mindfulness training, employees relax more, they experience more well-being and less stress and burnout. They sleep better and are more resilient. Mindful employees are also more creative, have better relationships in the workplace, and work better together.

"The mind is just like a muscle — the more you exercise it, the stronger it gets and the more it can expand."

IDOWU KOYENIKAN

But mindfulness is not a cure for all problems and certainly not a panacea. To avoid disappointment, it is important to have the right expectations.

–   Those who are mindful in life encounter problems just as often. The idea is not to simply sit back and meditate in order to "think away" the problems. On the contrary, by looking at problems mindfully, you just come closer to the core of the problem, but without your feelings overpowering you. Then you can take the bull by the horns in a much more purposeful way and solve the problem efficiently.
–   Integrating mindfulness into your life is not always obvious. This requires quite some discipline and new habits. It may also not become a stressor in itself if you don't try to practice mindfulness well or often enough.
–   Organizations or leaders should not impose mindfulness. It is not because you yourself as a manager are enthusiastic about the positive effects of mindfulness that this method will work for everyone. It is not a question of forcing your employees to attend mindfulness sessions. If you do, employees will only become control-motivated to develop mindfulness and the training will miss its purpose.

1.4   Personal intrinsic and extrinsic values

People find different things important in their life or in certain areas of life such as their work. Our values or goals determine how we see and perceive the world. They also have an impact on how we feel, how we think and what we do.

According to goal theory, striving for any goal already has a positive effect. Those who have specific, measurable, achievable, realistic, and time-bound (SMART) goals will be more committed than those who have no or only vague goals. But SDT nuances this story: not all values or goals have equally beneficial effects. According to SDT people can pursue two types of values, which clearly have different impacts:

– Extrinsically oriented employees are mainly concerned with the impression they make on the outside world. They view themselves through the eyes of others and constantly compare themselves with others. For them it is not about being financially well off per se, it's about being seen as successful by others. Extrinsically oriented people want to have more and more and are materialistic.
– Intrinsically oriented employees are primarily focused on realizing their intrinsic growth trend and want to grow not only personally, but also in their relationships with others. They are focused on "being there" rather than "having".

Extrinsic values	Intrinsic values
Some employees primarily seek or strive for extrinsic values:	Other employees primarily pursue intrinsic values:
– Financial success – Wealth: being rich and successful on a material level; – Appearance – Popularity: image, being known, being admired by many; – Power – Status: having a high position in an organization or in society; – Attractiveness: beautiful, attractive and sexy, meeting a beauty ideal.	– Personal development: developing talents, self-development, growth; – Social relationships: developing real, deep, open and authentic relationships; – Contribution to society: support charities, be in solidarity; – Health: being healthy, in good physical and mental condition.

Of course, having some financial means is needed to pay for your groceries and it is nice to exert a little influence on others. But those who focus too much on the pursuit of extrinsic values will come out disappointed. Research shows that the pursuit of extrinsic values is not satisfying at all. Because even if you succeed in achieving these extrinsic values, this will not fulfill your ABC. Pursuing extrinsic values at the expense of intrinsic values will frustrate your ABC.

"In fact, the fulfillment of psychological needs is a better predictor of daily happiness than money."

EDWARD F. DIENER

> **CASE**
>
> Lisa has a great job, nice colleagues, and works close to home. Every morning she leaves for work with a smile. Yet she is embarrassed when others ask her what she does. She works as a cleaning lady, and finds it a low-status job. If she could get over it, she would experience more joy in life. But at the moment she cannot. She thinks her image is still too important.
>
> Tom takes great pains to look good. Nice clothes, nice car. And yet, if one day people don't look at him with admiration when he gets out of his nice car, he wonders if there's something wrong with him. This often makes him feel very insecure.

WHAT IS IMPORTANT TO YOU IN LIFE? DO YOU WANT TO…

- be admired by your colleagues?
- have a high status among your friends?
- develop yourself?
- help people around you?
- be able to do something for society, such as consume less energy?

What if you are pursuing many extrinsic and few intrinsic values? Research shows that when employees place high importance on extrinsic values, they are less satisfied with their work and less engaged and autonomously motivated. They are more likely to experience burnout, have more problems in combining work and home, and are more likely to plan to leave their organization. Extrinsically oriented employees do little to no extra work for which they are not explicitly rewarded, such as helping out colleagues.

The pursuit of extrinsic values at work is also detrimental to life outside of work: those who pursue extrinsic values at work are less happy and satisfied with their lives in general. It causes anxiety, insecurity, depression, and a fragile self-image. Extrinsically oriented people also have more psychosomatic complaints like unexplained headaches and discomforting tensions in their back and shoulders, a greater risk of cardiovascular disease, and consume more cigarettes and alcohol.

Consequently, people who pursue extrinsic values live shorter lives.

CASE

Within a large IT company, each employees received a business diary, so everyone could tell which job level other employees had. The lower levels received a small diary with a plastic cover, the level above also got a small diary but with a leather cover, and the next level up got a big one with rings.

When staff members pulled out their diaries in a meeting, you could immediately see which function level you were dealing with. But also the phones on their desks, their cell phones, and the size of the computer screens differed according to their position in the organization. Of course, the company car also reflected their level: compact, mid-size, or large. And while board members and management flew business class, their lower-level colleagues who attended the same meetings flew economy.

Older people who, looking back on their lives, indicate that they have invested energy and time in extrinsic goals and were successful in doing so, are not necessarily more satisfied with their lives. On the contrary, those who realized extrinsic goals are more despondent around the end of their life and have more difficulty accepting death. Seniors who achieved mostly intrinsic goals in their lives, on the other hand, report more well-being and more death acceptance.

"You can buy a very beautiful dog,
but not the wagging of its tail."

JOSH BILLINGS

SUMMARY

CONSEQUENCES OF EXTRINSIC AND INTRINSIC VALUE PURSUIT

Extrinsic values	Intrinsic values
– Less well-being	– Higher well-being
– Less satisfied with work	– More self-actualization
– Less engagement	– More vitality
– More stress	– Better physical and mental health
– More burnout	– Fewer psychological problems
– More short-term satisfaction	– Less imbalance between work and
– More turnover	home
– More imbalance between work and home	– Less negative emotions such as fear, anger, and sadness
– More negative emotions, such as fear, anger and sadness	– More positive emotions such as pleasure and happiness
– More depression	– Less substance use
– More substance use (alcohol, cigarettes, drugs)	– Less depression
– More depression	
– More purchase addiction	
– More debts	

CASE

Quentin and Marie had started working together in a large electronics chain. Quentin worked in the northern city branch and Marie in the southern city branch. They were both looking forward to their new job. During their first month, they went through a sales training course organized by headquarters. They got to know the products and received advice from the best salespeople. Quentin's mentor urged him to keep his ears and eyes open as much as possible during training. This would help him to gain knowledge about the products and gain insight into the types of customers the chain of electronics attracted, so that he would be become better at really serving them. He attached great importance to intrinsic values such as self-development and helping others. Marie's mentor, on the other hand, emphasized a lot of extrinsic values. When Marie could properly master sales, their branch would perhaps sell the most of all. As a result, they would not only increase the organization's revenue but also receive an extra bonus. Although Quentin and Marie received the same training, it had a completely different effect. Marie did not seem to know the difference between the types of devices and several times she had to call in another salesperson for her administration. The atmosphere in her branch was tense. Quentin, on the other hand, walked around in his branch whistling and had no trouble finding the right match between customers' demands and the electronic devices on sale.

So it's important when you set up training to pay attention to the values you communicate.

- If you think about extrinsic values when learning, you will learn less deeply and experience more stress.
- If you pursue intrinsic values, you will absorb the learning material more deeply and remember and be able to use what you have learned.

Some nuances have to be made.

1. Many people overestimate the positive effects of extrinsic values. They think these values are important and achieving them will make them happy. And sometimes they do. Those who hold extrinsic values are more likely to have the feeling of *momentary happiness*, or, a good feeling after you have finished a piece of work, but which quickly fades away again and leaves employees left with a sense of emptiness and disappointment. This is why extrinsic values are so addictive: you want to live from one short-lived moment of happiness to the next. But then you miss out on the more lasting feelings of satisfaction and commitment that you do experience when you pursue intrinsic values.

2. Whether or not you *achieve your goals* does not matter. Do extrinsic values contribute less to happiness because they are harder to achieve? No. Even those who pursue and achieve extrinsic goals pay a price. Lawyers who work in a prestigious firm with a high salary get what they consider important. Despite this, they report more negative emotions, lower well-being and more alcohol use compared to lawyers who work in a non-profit sector.

3. A *match* between your goals and those of your environment does not necessarily lead to better work outcomes. It is often assumed that a fit or match between employees' values and those of the organization leads to the best results. But here too we have to distinguish between intrinsic and extrinsic values. Even matching extrinsic values between a person and their environment does not lead to better outcomes. Economics students who pursue extrinsic values do not feel as good about themselves and use more substances (e.g., alcohol, cigarettes, drugs), even though in their studies they often hear about the value of money and financial gain. This pattern was also found among law students: the well-being of highly success-ful students decreased in their first year of law school, mainly because they became more focused on achieving extrinsic goals.

So does money buy happiness?

It is often said that "money doesn't buy happiness". As is often the case, reality is more nuanced. Money can make us happy, especially if it ensures that we no longer have to worry about having a roof over our heads. People with little or no income are plagued by an all-consuming financial stress.
Additional financial resources then provide more security and relieve that stress. People who are wealthier and do not have to worry about day-to-day expenses gain much less with additional income in terms of happiness.

As soon as the pursuit of more money serves to satisfy materialistic goals, people experience markedly less well-being. And this is true for both people with high and low incomes. Also among poor emigrated Chinese rural workers, it was found that realizing material aspirations predicted less well-being. The pursuit of extrinsic, materialistic values distracts from the fulfillment of the ABC.

People have several reasons to make money:

The pursuit of financial stability in and of itself is not detrimental. Money increases your well-being when you use it to fulfill your own and others' ABC needs. For example, decent housing stimulates your needs of autonomy and competence. In addition, supporting your loved ones will also contribute to the need for belongingness, because it strengthens your relationships.

When you want to earn a fair wage for your work, or have an income to stand on your own two feet, pursue hobbies, or help people in need, you will be more likely to fulfill your ABC and therefore experience more well-being and less stress. The pursuit of money to help others fosters meaningful and valuable relationships. Having a positive impact on the lives of others increases your sense of connection and competence.

Wanting to make money to take pride in who you are, outshine others, or spend money impulsively will frustrate your ABC. Earning money to attract attention and brag about it can create long-term feelings of pressure, isolation, and incompetence. This diminishes your well-being and increases your stress.

"I'm not materialistic. I believe in presents from the heart, like a drawing that a child does."

VICTORIA BECKHAM

WHAT ABOUT YOU?

Why do you (like to) earn money?

— to build up a financial reserve;
— to support friends and family;
— to know that I'm getting a fair return for the work that I do;
— to prove to myself that I am successful;
— to enjoy luxurious things (e.g., cars, houses, art);
— to impulsively buy what I want;
— to prove to myself that I am not a failure.

1.5 Different cultures

Some criticize SDT for being a Western theory, because it places much emphasis on autonomy. Autonomy is mainly at stake in individualistic cultures and not so much in collective cultures, such as those in Asia, where the individual is considered more part of a group.

However, this criticism is based on a definition of autonomy as independence and being able to decide everything for oneself without regard for others. This differs considerably from the way SDT looks at autonomy, as a feeling that you have to do things voluntarily and not "against your will".

Research confirms that SDT endures in a wide variety of countries or cultures ranging from South Korea, Russia, Turkey to the United States. In all of these cultures, people feel better about themselves as soon as they are more autonomously motivated. This implies that the fulfillment of our ABC is necessary for our well-being, even in collectivist cultures.

This is also true in the work context. Deci and colleagues examined the fulfillment of the ABC among employees in American and Bulgarian companies. They found, in both cultures, that the extent to which supervisors supported their employees' ABC predicted the satisfaction of their ABC. This, in turn, benefited employee engagement and well-being. Employees' autonomy was thus important not only in a capitalist culture like the United States, but also in (then) socialist Bulgaria. SDT is thus relevant to companies with different nationalities in the workplace.

"... basic psychological need satisfactions were among the strongest predictors of positive affect, wellness and happiness across the world."

EDWARD DECI & RICHARD RYAN

WHAT ABOUT YOU?

Do you work with people from a different cultural background?

- Do you think they have different needs?
- Do you motivate them in a different way?

SUMMARY

- Some people are lucky and satisfy their ABC naturally. They instinctively maneuver themselves into situations in which they can fulfill their ABC needs, see more opportunities for need fulfillment, and allow others to help them.
- Others experience more pressure from the environment, put more pressure or pursue values that offer less opportunities to fulfill their ABC.

So being open to opportunities to fulfill your needs is important. For those seeking to motivate others, it is important to remember that:

- you'd best differentiate between the different types of motivation;
- it is best to fulfill the ABC in all your employees. It increases autonomous motivation for everyone;
- you'd best avoid ABC frustration in everyone.

But autonomous motivation and the fulfillment of your ABC are not predominantly determined by people's personality. Instead, environmental factors have a far greater impact. We discuss in the following chapters how this works.

2. THE IDEAL SALARY ACCORDING TO SDT

WHAT ABOUT YOU?

- How important is your salary to you?
- Do you get a bonus? Is it fair and just? Are you happy with it? Or would it like to be higher?
- Have you ever received an award (e.g., best salesperson, employee of the month)?
  - How did that make you feel?
  - How did you feel when someone else got the recognition?
- Do you ever give compliments to colleagues, coworkers or your manager?
- What would you do if you won the lottery? Or if a basic wage was introduced?
  - Would you still go to work?
  - Would you still continue to do the same job?
  - Or would you finally pursue your dreams?

" If somebody claims that you can achieve anything with money, you can be sure that he has never had any."

ARISTOTLE ONASSIS

Do we continue to work when we win the lottery and no longer need the money? That is a question that probes autonomous work motivation: how enjoyable, interesting or meaningful do you find your work? Would you still want to do it if there is no reward in return?

Unfortunately, the chances of "Win for Life" are slim and an unconditional universal basic income has not yet been introduced, save a few experiments. So we will continue to work for the money.

Important questions then are:

- How motivating is your wage or salary?
- Does it increase your autonomous motivation?
- Or do your salary and that cool bonus rather increase your controlled motivation?

A wage or salary is an essential part of paid employment. You give your time and energy to your employer, and he pays you for it. Wages are therefore a "manifest" or "obvious" reason for leaving work. Other benefits of work are much less noticeable. But work also, for example, gives structure to your day, allows you to build an identity, makes you contribute to a larger whole, and makes social contact possible.

In addition to salary and possibly fringe benefits or bonuses, we can also look more broadly at rewards in general. Just think of compliments, feedback, a staff party, promotions, a bottle of wine, borrowing the truck from work for your move. These are all (external) rewards. How can they satisfy the ABC and have an optimal motivating effect?

2.1 Intrinsic motivation decreases due to rewards: the crowding-out effect

The ideal pay:

- does justice to their performance;
- is not too high;
- but certainly not too low either;
- feels fair;
- meets their ABC so that their autonomous motivation increases and controlled motivation decreases.

It is not easy to properly reward your employees for their work. You want to avoid situations where pay makes employees less motivated for their work. This is a real risk. As Deci's puzzle experiment shows (see Part 1), students were less motivated to solve puzzles once they had received money for this intrinsically motivating task.

The tailor in the parable below experienced something similar: A tailor opened a new store. On the very first day, angry boys started throwing stones at the display case and causing damage. The tailor did not know what to do and slept badly that night. Repairing the display case after the stone strike would cost him a lot of money. When the bad boys reappeared the next day, the tailor gave each of them a small piece of silver. "Here," he said, "because you are making an effort to make my store known, I reward you with a piece of silver." The next day, the boys came back, and threw stones again. The tailor came out and said that a piece of silver was actually too much and that he would only give them piece of bronze. The boys left, a little disappointed, with the piece of bronze. The next day instead of a piece of bronze they got a penny. "Why do we only get a penny?" they asked. "First we got silver, then bronze, and now only a penny?". "I have nothing left…" sighed the tailor. "Do you now really think that for one more cent we will throw stones at your showcase?" the boys shouted indignantly! And the tailor replied: "Well, then you'll no longer do it, right?" And so it was done.

Deci's puzzle experiment and the tailor's story illustrate the crowding-out effect: intrinsic motivation is pushed away by extrinsic rewards. By giving a reward, the tailor managed to bring the stone throwing under "control" of the reward. Then he gradually reduced this reward. And along with the reward, intrinsic motivation decreased. Instead of double as much motivation (intrinsic "liking to throw" and external motivation "throwing for the reward"), first the intrinsic motivation disappeared. And then when this reward also disappeared (i.e., external motivation), there was no motivation left at all.

Also in the work context we often give and receive rewards. Consider, for example:

- a bonus for each signed contract;
- handing out awards for best performing team;
- appreciation for a successful project;
- extra money or drink for work well done.

Often, these rewards are not consistent enough to keep up employees' external motivation. Say, one year, the entire department receives an extraordinary bonus or premium, but the following year, the budget no longer allows for such extra pay due to an economic downturn or the money goes to another department. What is the impact of this on work motivation?

WHAT ABOUT YOU?

How do you feel about your salary?

- Is your base pay high enough?
- Does your salary or bonus motivate you to work harder or better?
- What rewards motivate you the most?

SDT argues that some rewards trigger the crowding-out effect faster than others. Here too the ABC plays an important role, as the effect of rewards depends on two opposing influences on our ABC.

First, rewards create less autonomy and more control.
On the one hand, rewards can frustrate the need for autonomy. Rewards cause you to stop volunteering to work ("I want to commit to this task, because I like it or see merit in the task itself"). Instead, they create a sense of pressure ("I have to do this task to get the reward"). The reward is so central that the "overjustification effect" begins to come into play: when you are rewarded for an interesting

or fun activity, you will attribute the reason for your behavior to the reward and not to your interest or pleasure. The result is that you feel controlled and develop external motivation. The quality of your performance deteriorates and you feel less good.

CASE

Nora is a passionate hobby photographer. She is talented and loves to really get to know her clients in order to capture them perfectly. After a few years of doing photography as a sideline, she gave up her regular job and started her big adventure: her own photography business. She quickly attracted clients and customers and started earning more money than in her old job. Whenever a customer called, she could already hear the cash register ringing. But with the numbers in her accounts rising, she began to feel more and more like she was becoming less creative. She found herself under pressure to take on more customers and give them exactly what they wanted. It was nice that she had been able to transform her hobby into a profession, but her need for autonomy became more and more frustrated.

Second, rewards provide more competence, as they provide more information

On the other hand, rewards can satisfy the need for competence. If rewards offer correct feedback, they mainly have an informative function. A nice compliment from a colleague gives you the feeling that you have done well. That makes you feel better about yourself and perform better.

CASE

Jeff is a passionate carpenter. He enjoys placing wooden gates perfectly and love to give his customers advice about their windows. Sometimes he would get a tip from customers, say 5 or 10 euros. Not a large amount of money, but Jeff enjoyed the appreciation that his customers gave him in this way.

So what is the secret recipe for rewarding employees, without their high-quality, autonomous motivation suffering? How can you better motivate employees who are poorly or not well motivated for their work through their pay?

The answer lies in the ABC: focus on rewards that strengthen the ABC rather than frustrate it. Try to be informative without being controlling. When the salary, compliment or feedback comes across as coercive, evaluative or manipulative, it will have the opposite effect on the needs for autonomy and competence, and thus on the autonomous motivation and well-being of your employees.

WHAT ABOUT YOU?

How do you experience the rewards you receive?

- — Are they informative?
- — Or do you experience them more as controlling?

And you as a manager?

- — Do you use rewards to try to put pressure on your employees so that they will do the same next time?
- — Or do you give purely informative rewards to give them feedback or to express your gratitude?
- — What can you do to make your rewards less controlling and more informative?

In what follows, we discuss how aspects of the reward and the broader reward system themselves help determine whether a reward is more likely to be seen as controlling or informative.

2.2 What should you be looking for when giving a reward?

From an SDT perspective, not every reward is the same. To ensure that rewards are truly motivating, it is important to take into account the following five questions:

1. Is the reward tangible, material, and conspicuous? Or is it verbal, non-material, and discrete?
2. Is the reward expected or unexpected?
3. What is the relation between the reward and the task for which you are rewarding?
4. Are you rewarding for a simple or a complex task?
5. How fair is the reward?

Each of these factors provides useful information about whether the reward will achieve its goal. Namely, more autonomous motivation, better performance and higher well-being.

2.2.1 Is the reward tangible, material, and conspicuous? Or verbal, non-material, and discrete?

Some rewards are very visible and tangible. A box of chocolates from your boss for New Year, a fruit basket for good work, your year-end bonus, or a cash envelope are examples of a tangible reward.

Other rewards are intangible. Positive feedback or compliments are verbal rewards. They can leave a deep impression, but are actually fleeting. A good conversation with your supervisor, a pat on the back, but also your salary paid into your bank account without you being aware of it are less conspicuous rewards.

WHAT ABOUT YOU?

— Do you like getting a gift from your boss?
— Do you like getting compliments?

- Are there any compliments that only make you feel more stressed?
- Are most of your rewards tangible or intangible?

What about you as a manager?

- Do you occasionally give gifts or compliments to your employees?
- Have you ever given a bottle of champagne to your employees because they performed well?

Several meta-analyses show that the "crowding-out effect" or the effect of rewards on intrinsic motivation is a lot greater for tangible rewards than for verbal rewards. Tangible rewards are more noticeable and therefore you will attribute your behavior to the reward sooner. Here then emerges the undermining effect. With rewards that are more discrete and/or verbal, this chance is lower.

Notably, compliments, an often-used form of verbal reward, can undermine autonomous motivation as well. Compliments such as, "You are a brilliant employee. I knew I could count on you to finish this project in the evenings!" can trigger internal compulsion and provoke internal pressure. Who doesn't want to be a reliable employee? It gets worse when employees display a certain behavior (e.g., answering emails late at night) just to get recognition or approval in the form of a compliment. After all, this means that employees are under external pressure. Motivational compliments and feedback try to avoid such internal or external pressure and focus on strengthening the employees' competence by describing the observed behavior and express the positive emotions of seeing this.

"A drop of tenderness is more than money and power."

BUDDHA

CASE

At a large company based in Brussels, employees are encouraged to use a "feedback tool". The idea is that after a nice meeting, a pleasant conversation, or after someone had helped you out, you could use this tool to give the colleague in question feedback. The tool was announced with much fanfare and its use was stimulated via the intranet. Initially, the feedback you gave also went to your manager. After several complaints that this came across as very controlling, this feature was removed. But even then, the tool had little success. It was barely used, if at all. By making the feedback so visual, not only for the colleagues concerned, but for the others as well, the feedback became much more tangible, and its spontaneous effect was lost. After a while, the expensive feedback program was scrapped.

TIPS

These compliments are best avoided:	These compliments support the ABC:
– "Well done! Exactly what you'd expect from someone with your level." – "I will be extremely impressed if by tonight you have all these documents sorted." – "I knew I could also count on you in the evenings to finish this project." – "So nice that you don't mind my yelling and ranting and raving at all." – "I have not received most of the data yet, but you're doing it really well. And if you keep it up, I can use yours."	– "You did this super well as it respects the standard of quality we have put forward together." – "Thanks, the results of your work are really helping me along." – "Excellent, keep up the good work, this really helps the team." – "What a top performance!" – "My friend, you are a colleague we can count on." – "What wonderful progress you have made." – "So nice to work with you together."

2.2.2 Is the reward expected or unexpected?

Many rewards are announced in advance: Already at the start of your job, you know exactly how much you will earn and whether or not a bonus is possible. The title "Top seller of the year" and that end-of-year-bonus are annual recurring phenomena.

Sometimes a reward comes unexpectedly: flowers from your client at his farewell, a bottle of wine from your boss after you've met a deadline, lunch with a colleague you want to thank, or a compliment from your otherwise rather reserved colleague are all rewards you didn't see coming from afar.

Expected rewards more easily frustrate the need for autonomy. Unexpected rewards do so less. The mechanism behind this is simple: if you are not expecting a reward while you are working on the task, this reward cannot affect the intrinsic motivation for the task. Thus, you therefore don't get the impression that your behavior is "controlled" by the reward.

Unexpected rewards do provide clear positive feedback about your performance and thus increase your sense of competence. In other words, you can "reward" someone for doing something good, without their knowing it in advance.

CASE

Ken has brought in a big client. It is not customary to reward salespeople for this, but because this client is very special, Ken received a bonus. Ken had not expected that, but was very happy about it. He could use the extra money. In the prospecting phase, he had not at all taken into account the fact that he could be rewarded for this, so the whole process had gone autonomously and well. The bonus made him feel even more competent as a salesman. His motivation got a boost. But he still had some big customers in mind...

Of course, there is a catch here. Employees can begin to expect "unexpected" rewards if they occur frequently. Will dinner after a successful project or a box of chocolates after a published article become a tradition? That's fine, but know that such expectations also increase the pressure to get the reward (and thus potentially diminish the satisfaction of the need for autonomy).

CASE

James is a consultant and also a much sought-after lecturer at several universities. He enjoys teaching and finds it very useful to pass on all his knowledge and expertise to students. Each year an award is presented to the best teacher. The past few years he had missed out on the award, and it went to more experienced and well-known teachers. But this year, to his great surprise, he won. What an honor, but it also stressed James out. He wondered what he had to do now to win next year's award. Because other teachers had won the prize several years in a row. All of a sudden, he noticed that being "popular" became more important to him than passing on knowledge. He also thought that perhaps he should make his exams a little less difficult, to increase his chances of receiving the award.

WHAT ABOUT YOU?

— Have you ever received an unexpected reward?
— Have you stopped surprising your employees with a reward, because you noticed that after a while they started to take it for granted?
— Do you brighten up when a surprise suddenly appears on your desk?

2.2.3 Is the reward dependent on the task?

Rewards are not always given under the same conditions. Ryan and colleagues list a number of possibilities:

- *Not dependent:* You get your reward independently of your performance on the task.
- *Engagement dependent*: You get your reward because you started with the task.
- *Completion dependent:* You get your reward for completing the task.
- *Result dependent:* You get your reward when you achieve a certain result.

A) *Your reward is not dependent on the task*

You get your reward independent of how long or how well you worked on the task. When the team with the best result receives a bonus, you as an individual employee do not always have impact on whether or not you get the bonus. Try as you might, if everyone else in your team just sits back and relaxes, you won't get the reward.

What happens to your autonomy and competence then? Rewards that are not related to your performance don't put any pressure on you, but they also don't give any information about how well you did. Therefore, this form of reward has little positive impact on your motivation, well-being, and performance.

B) *Engagement dependent: your reward depends on whether or not you are engaged in the task*

With an engagement dependent reward, you receive the reward simply because you started the task and worked on it. You do not have to finish the task or reach a certain level of performance to receive the reward. Working on it is enough. A monthly base pay or an hourly wage are classic examples of this. When you have completed the hours, you will be paid a wage.

These rewards provide little feedback on how well you performed the task, but can frustrate the need for autonomy to some extent. The risk exists that you are no longer really concerned with the task, but mainly with the reward that should follow. Then, intrinsic motivation has no chance to come about. You do not enjoy the task and perform less well.

CASE

Sara is a cleaner during the summer holidays. The factory where she works has a fully continuous system. So she also worked on weekends and Sundays. The fact that she was expected to work on a national holiday (on a Saturday) was a windfall: she received her weekend bonus and a bonus for working on a public holiday. All day long, she and the other students joked about how much they earned per hour, or even per minute. Take a coffee break? That means so many extra euros. During lunch, the French fries they had ordered paid for themselves. But the generous compensation didn't make for a generous performance: most of the regular staff was at home that day, so they took extra-long breaks.

While engagement dependent rewards do not always have positive effects, research shows that a high base salary – which is a form of engagement dependent reward – does motivate intrinsically. After all, employees see this as an expression of appreciation by the organization.

Why is the basic salary for permanent employees motivating while a commitment-related reward for job students has the opposite effect? The explanation lies in the degree to which this reward is or is not conspicuous, as described above. A student usually chooses to work during vacations or on weekends to earn extra money. The content of the work is often less important. Given that earning money is their main goal and still something relatively new, students tend to know every day, or even every hour, how much they earn. For permanent employees it is different: although salary plays a role in the choice of a job, content still comes first. When you don't have much financial stress, you are less focused on your pay, as long as it appears in your bank account each month.

Rewarding employees for their commitment to certain tasks also brings a lot of unintended negative effects. Gubler and colleagues conducted a study on this in an industrial laundry. Employees in a laundry were often absent and management aimed to use a material reward to boost attendance. It turned out that the reward had a positive effect on the attendance of employees who had previously been regularly absent. So far, so good.

But there were also drawbacks. The reward program gave rise to strategic behavior. Those who thought they had no chance of winning the reward that month were even more likely to be absent the rest of the month. The positive effect also proved to be short-lived. As soon as the program was stopped, attendance figures dropped again. Pithy detail: not only the employees who were frequently absent before the intervention were often absent again. Employees who were almost always present before the program also increasingly failed to show up for work. And they worked 8% less efficiently than before the program.

In short, the entire program had major financial consequences for the laundry. The managers had expected the cost of the reward ($75 per month) to easily "pay for itself" in increased attendance and productivity gains. But the entire program turned out to cost more than it brought in.

C) *Completion dependent: you receive a reward when you finish your task*

Did you completely finish the task? Then you get the completion dependent reward, independent of the quality of the delivered work. Movers get the amount agreed upon once all the items are in the new house. A gardener gets his quote paid when the job is done. Quality control can only be done after the day's work or not at all. Have all the boxes been moved to your new place? Are all the items intact? If the flowers don't come out or the trees won't grow, is this the gardener's fault or is it the fertilization of the soil?

What about autonomy and competence?

- Completion dependent rewards put a certain amount of pressure. Here too, you run the risk that employees are no longer focused on the task itself, but rather on getting the reward. This gets in the way of the need for autonomy.
- But completion dependent rewards also imply that you have reached a certain level of competence. So they can satisfy the need for competence. That (implicit) positive feedback can partially compensate for the negative effect of perceived control. Unfortunately, this compensation is rarely, if ever, complete. As a result, this form of reward will again undermine intrinsic motivation and therefore their well-being and performance.

> **CASE**
>
> John is glad that the work is done again. In one day, the garden house was completely assembled. Nice work, but actually he found that it could be better. Unfortunately, his boss had urged him that everything had to be ready today. He had therefore worked a little faster than he would have liked, and the gutter drain was not completely closed. It had been done according to the instructions and it wouldn't leak for the first year. Yet John knew from experience that it could be done better. But time was running out, and so "finished quickly" earned more appreciation than "perfectly done".

D) *Result-dependent reward: how you are rewarded depends on the result*

A result-dependent reward is the one you get only if you achieve a certain result, a predefined criterion or a certain level. This type of reward is perhaps the best-known form of the classic "pay-for-performance" system. You get a higher salary and/or bigger bonus as soon as you meet certain performance standards.

Examples include bonuses for top managers and rewards for winning contracts or selling a certain number of products.

CASE

Wim, working in the HR department of a home furniture company, searched in vain for new engineers for the design department. In order to attract new people, he launched a contest. Whoever brought in new people received 250 dollars upon recruitment. If the new force stayed at least six months, they could compete for a trip to Rome. Even with this system, it was not easy to find good workers.

Rewarding someone when they do a good job gives a motivation boost, doesn't it? Almost everyone considers result-dependent rewards "logical" and "efficient".

- "When employees do their best and achieve the set goals, we can pay them well for that, can't we?"
- "If the results are not met, then we reward them less."

But there's a catch.

- When rewards are linked to performance, employees often experience this as controlling. After all, they have to meet a certain standard to get the reward, and this frustrates their need for autonomy.
- This negative effect may be somewhat offset by the fact that result-oriented rewards also provide information about their competence. If they get the reward, they have made an excellent performance. This satisfies their need for competence.

However, several meta-analyses show that this positive effect does not outweigh the increased pressure. Result-dependent rewards elicit controlled motivation, decreasing the quality of people's motivation. Employees' well-being is therefore compromised, and the very best performance paradoxically fails to materialize.

> **CASE**
>
> Peter is a top salesman. After two months, he has already reached his target for the quarter. So his bonus is safe. He still has a few more customers on his list, but he is facing a dilemma. If he has them sign another offer in the next month, it will not affect his salary. If he waits another month, this will contribute to the next evaluation period. Will he serve his customers as quickly as possible and with the best possible service? That would be better for them and the organization! But for his own financial situation, he would better make them wait a while.

In addition, result-dependent rewards also have negative side effects. Employees who want to get the result-dependent bonus at all costs think in the short term: how can they maximize their return with as little effort as possible? This is often at the expense of things that are not immediately rewarded but are valuable for the organization in the long term, such as knowledge sharing, helping colleagues, and taking on extra projects.

Already a decade ago, research pointed at the negative consequences of an extreme "pay-for-performance" program within the telecommunications industry. Here, after a two-month training program, employees worked entirely on commission. They received no base pay, so their pay was completely and directly dependent on their performance. As a result, three-quarters of the salespeople who were remunerated in this way had left the company within a year. A sky-high cost to the organization!

> **CASE**
>
> Tim is paid monthly for the number of families he can convince to switch to his green energy supplier. He strongly believes that this is where the future lies, and because he speaks with passion

and knowledge, he manages to get a lot of families to switch. As a result, he receives a nice (yet variable) salary every month. He often receives questions from those new customers, weeks after the switch. He would like to respond to them, but the system only "pays" him for bringing in new customers, not for aftercare. Tim regrets this, but no matter how useful he thinks the after-sales service is, he focuses on bringing in new customers. A year later, he learns that a large number of the customers he had acquired are switching back to their previous – not so green – supplier because they provide better customer support. Tim is crestfallen about the organization where he works, and feels his enthusiasm for the job is decreasing.

WHAT ABOUT YOU? IS YOUR BASE PAY HIGH ENOUGH?

- What are you being paid for?
  - Just for being there?
  - Or do you have to complete certain tasks?
  - Maybe you even have to meet certain standards or expectations?
  - Does your pay depend partly or entirely on your performance?
  - Do you get an extra reward if you meet your goals?
- Do you sometimes experience pressure to achieve your goals just for the sake of an extra pay/reward?

And you as a manager?

- Do you find it logical to reward your employees when they reach their goals?
- Do you sometimes feel that your employees leave things out for which they are not being rewarded, such as working together or helping each other?
- Would you like to reward your employees even more when they do things well, such as showing up for work on time or being less absent?

2.2.4 What do you reward? Simple versus complex tasks

Performance is a broad concept. As there are different types of tasks, there are also different types of performance.

With simple tasks, the focus is primarily on the *quantity of the performance*. The task in itself does not require much training or skills and you can usually complete it quickly. Sorting beer bottles, unloading boxes, sorting chocolates, the daily maintenance of a gymnasium, and directing customers to the right floor are all relatively simple tasks.

In complex tasks, the focus is on the *quality of the performance*. The task is difficult, not obvious to solve, and requires a certain effort. Examples are building a passive house, devising a personalized marketing plan, giving advice to your patients or writing a book.

It has been 40 years now since several meta-analyses showed that rewards improve performance on simple tasks and reduce performance on more complex tasks.

– Those who receive a bonus or reward for "doing more of the same" in a simple task, perform this task faster and thus put up a better performance.
– If, on the other hand, the work is complex, then a reward will merely cause the quality of your performance to drop. You make more mistakes and cut corners. It is more difficult to be creative and innovative when you are under pressure and/or are eagerly awaiting that reward. A bonus per site completed? Then there is a greater chance that the insulation shell around the house is not completely airtight. Earning more if the marketing plan gets done faster? You may consider providing each of your customers with a standard plan. Speed does not go hand in hand with quality work. And employees will also find it less fun to work on these complex projects if they do it for the reward.

So do you want quality, innovation, and creativity? Then a focus on intrinsic motivation or perceived meaningfulness is much better for motivating than extrinsic rewards.

Glucksberg studied this phenomenon as early as in 1962. He had people come up with a solution to the "candle problem". The idea is that you attach a candle to the wall without candle wax dripping onto the floor. In the complex version, people are given a box with thumbtacks, a candle and some matches. In an attempt to find the solution, they then try to melt the candle with candle wax against the wall, use the thumbtacks to make a shelf, etc. It takes a while for them to realize that they can use the thumbtack box to make a candle holder that can be attached to the wall using thumbtacks. When a reward is promised, people take even longer, on average, to arrive at this solution. In the simple version of this task, people are given a box, a pile of thumbtacks, a candle and some matches. Then it becomes easy! The box is now no longer seen as the holder for the thumbtacks, but as a possible candlestick. In this easy version, whether or not you promise a reward has no negative effect on the speed with which people solve the problem.

Simple tasks are not always autonomously motivating. This may be due to their repetitive nature, their simplicity, because they are less interesting or fun, or because employees do not always see the value or point of them. In our workshops participants often cite the fact that they find it difficult to motivate themselves to do their administration or to take the annual inventory. Is it a good idea to reward employees for those simple tasks and thus "buy off" their motivation? That may be a solution. But of course it is much better to make these tasks fun or meaningful, as we discussed in Part 1.

WHAT ABOUT YOU?

— Do you make the distinction between simple and complex tasks?
— Do you reward differently depending on the complexity?

2.2.5 Justice

An important consideration when giving a reward, in any form, is fairness. It is important that employees feel that rewards are handed out in a fair manner:

- either because they are getting a fair share of the cake. We also call this distributive justice;
- or because the procedures followed to distribute rewards are fair and transparent. This is called procedural justice.

CASE

A large technology company awards its annual bonuses in two ways. On the one hand, there are clear procedures and goals, and there is clear and transparent communication around the bonuses, both for the group and for the individual targets. Procedural fairness is high. In addition, each executive has a bag of money with which he or she could play Santa Claus. Bonuses and promotions are then awarded completely arbitrarily. The only criteria that applies is favoritism or nepotism. Those who get nothing often felt treated unfairly. Those who are in good standing with the manager were lucky, but even they experience stress, because they don't even know what they had to do to get a bonus. Needless to say, this system causes stress and does not contribute to better performance or motivation.

TIPS

Do you want to reward your employees, and at the same time want them to:

- be and remain autonomously motivated?
- deliver top performance?
- feel good about themselves?
- experience little stress?

And do you also want this effect to spread over time?

Then a fair compensation that is not directly dependent on performance, together with an autonomy-supporting workplace, is the optimal combination. Especially for more complex tasks.

Do you still want to reward your employees for their performance? Then know that rewards produce the best results and the least damage when they are:

— unexpected,
— task-independent,
— non-controlling, and
— informative.

If, on the other hand, you want to improve performance for simple repetitive work, you might consider working with performance-based pay. It will then, mainly in the short term (though not in the long term), increase the quantity (though not the quality) of the work. But it will stimulate neither autonomous motivation nor the well-being of your employees.

Incidentally, do you want to not only respond to the needs for autonomy and competence, but also increase connection? Then consider rewarding the entire team or organization when a team achievement is reached.

CASE

An international software company organizes a citywide award every year and, if global business results are good, it organizes a city trip. Everyone is invited, from the cleaning lady to the highest executive. Many companies provide such trips only for salespeople because they are directly responsible for sales, but this company recognizes the individual contribution of all employees. The trip lasts three days: departure on Thursday

---

afternoon, return home on Saturday evening. So it's half private and half work time. How do they determine whether the trip will take place? In the communal coffee room there is a see-through tube. Every time a deal is signed, Operations fills this tube with confetti. Everyone can follow progress. As soon as the line with "city trip" is covered with confetti, the trip goes ahead. Also important: it is on a voluntary basis, no one is obliged to come along. Since there are fun team activities organized, this also benefits connection, involvement, and togetherness. In this way this organization involves all employees in its success in a fun way.

3. ABC-PROOF JOB DESIGN

- What do you like about your job? What aspects give you wings?
- What eats up energy and would you rather lose than have?
- Is your job still identical to the one in which you started?
- Have you ever made changes to your job? What did you do?
- Have you ever made changes to your employees' tasks?

People have a variety of reasons for choosing a particular job. We all have different preferences. For some, a job as an IT technician or gardener is a dream come true. For others, physical labor in all weather conditions is absolute horror and there is nothing more fun than helping customers with their questions about their new phone. A range of tasks that is autonomously motivating for one person is not so for another.

But it's not just the content of the tasks – the way the job is organized also plays a big role in how motivating the work is. The way a job is designed, or "constructed", plays a large role. In this chapter, we look at how you can (re)design jobs in a motivating way.

3.1 What is job design?

The way jobs are designed indicates how tasks, activities, and responsibilities are organized. Job design thus describes what jobs look like and what characteristics they have.

For example, consider the following furniture-making start-up that makes cabinets and chairs. For each cabinet, shelves must be cut to size, put together and painted. Frank, the owner of the company, knows that his employees are motivated carpenters with a passion for wood.

But how should he shape the respective jobs? Should he choose to create a separate department for sawing, assembling, and painting? And will he have his employees make chairs as well as cabinets? Or will he choose to have his employees make either chairs or cabinets, but from start to finish?

	Sawing Department	Assembling Department	Painting Department
Department of chairs	Sewing planks for chairs	Assembling planks for chairs	Painting chairs
Department of cupboards	Sewing planks for cupboards	Assembling planks for cupboards	Painting cupboards

Which choice would you make? In what kind of job would you mostly want to work?

Option 1: Would you prefer to become an expert in sawing, painting or assembling? You choose in advance which of the three tasks suits you best. You then receive the necessary training in order to specialize. You get the chance to work not only on chairs, but also on cabinets. A disadvantage is that you can only do one task: sawing, painting, *or* assembling. So you play a role in the beginning, middle *or* end of the process. You have little impact on what you get your hands on as an assembler or how it's sawn and painted. This is finished by your colleagues.

Option 2: Or do you prefer to completely finish a whole piece of furniture, a whole chair or cabinet? You will then receive training in making chairs or cabinets and learn how to saw, paint, and assemble. You make furniture from start to finish. A disadvantage is that you always make the same type of furniture over and over again. And you will probably be just a little bit better at, say, painting than sawing.

If Frank chooses option 1 and establishes a sawmill, an assembly department, and a paint department, he chooses Taylorist jobs. His employees will have to do the same activities over and over again. Employees can quickly learn the necessary skills and the machines they need to master are limited. The disadvantage of these jobs is that they are rather repetitive and tedious, precisely because there is little to learn in them. Such jobs often start from a Theory X approach: employees are primarily motivated by strictly checking whether they are performing their tasks correctly and by rewarding them financially for outstanding performance (e.g., piecework).

If Frank chooses option 2 and creates one department for chairs and one for cabinets, then his employees have a job with a lot of variation, in which they get feedback from their work and can solve problems themselves. In short, their jobs are more motivating in themselves. This closely resembles a Theory Y approach.

3.2 Motivating work contains many job resources or energy resources

Motivating work contains many "job resources" or energy sources. These are positive aspects of the work that really motivate many employees.

– *Feedback*: You get feedback from your work itself. When boards are not cut properly, they don't fit together. At assembly, you immediately notice this and you can adjust your way of working. When one employee is sawing and the other assembles, there is a delay in this feedback. With many incorrectly sawn boards as a result. The communication needed to rectify the error is not always smooth and may lead to conflicts.

- *Variation or skill utilization*: Those who work on the chairs or cabinets are allowed to do different things: sawing, assembling, and painting. Every day is different. This is motivating and also helps the organization. Someone who is familiar with different areas can switch more quickly and can also be deployed elsewhere when colleagues are ill, on sick leave, or when the organization changes. What if the painting is outsourced to keep up with demand? Variation ensures agile, flexible organizations and multi-deployable employees who have to worry little about job security: there is always a job for them to do!

- *Task Identity*: Those who are allowed to complete a task from start to finish know what they are doing and see the bigger picture. This is completely different in a Taylorist approach: there you are merely a small cog. Your work may be important, but you do not have a view of the total product, so that you may question the usefulness of your work.

- *Task Significance*: In a motivating way of organizing you also see the importance of your task for others. You don't just do monotonous work, you understand why your work is important. The joiner not only sees a nice row of sawed-off boards, but also a beautiful set of chairs. Knowing that it's quickly sold to a newlywed couple who find the chairs perfect, makes task significance even more clear.

- *Autonomy*: In a motivating job design, employees also have more decision-making power. For example, you can decide in which order to do tasks, what you need a little more time for and where you can work faster. You can choose your own methods. Autonomy enables you to organize your work better or more easily and produce higher quality work. So you can respond better to small problems or changes.

These positive characteristics in the work, or "energy sources", contribute to the fulfillment of the ABC. As a result, employees with motivating work have more energy and are less exhausted. A meta-analysis confirmed these results: each of the basic needs is satisfied when energy sources are present in the job. Each of these basic needs are then in turn important for employees' well-being, attitudes, and performance.

Note: In the above example of the furniture factory, we were looking directly at a very drastic change in the way we organize. Such a major change is not always possible or desirable. As a manager or HR consultant, you work in an organization with a certain organizational chart. This does not always allow you to completely redesign tasks. But within the team or even within each task package, you can investigate how you can make jobs more motivating.

CASE

During her internship in an HR department, Krista was initially only allowed to attend the selection interviews and write the reports. Fascinating, but after a while this became a bit boring. She discussed this with her internship supervisor Samira. Initially, Samira did not pay much attention to Krista's concerns, because it was the work that they had agreed upon, and the other interns found enough challenge in attending and writing the reports. Krista continued to attend the interviews, and afterwards, besides the standard report, she also gave Samira substantive feedback. She described the strengths and weaknesses of each candidate and gave feedback on the process. After evaluating this extra input, Samira saw that Krista's input did add value to the entire application process and invited her to take more responsibility in subsequent interviews. In the years that followed, the interns' job design was also enriched. Both the interns and the organization benefited.

In the example above, Krista's job is expanded: she can do more varied things, gets more autonomy and therefore her task identity and task significance improve.

WHAT ABOUT YOU? HOW ABOUT THE MOTIVATIONAL CHARACTERISTICS OF YOUR JOB?

— How often do you get feedback from your supervisor or colleagues?
— Do you have enough variation or do you often have to perform the same tasks?
— How is your work part of the bigger picture?
— Do you see how your work has a positive impact on people, also outside the organization?
— Are you allowed to decide where and when to work (e.g., in your schedule, flexible hours)?
— Are you allowed to choose your own way of working? Can you decide which tasks to work on?

And you as a manager?

— How is the work structured in your company? Is the focus on short-cycle tasks or do you opt for more motivating work?
— If employees feel little autonomous motivation, do you take a critical look at the range of tasks?
— What does the latest employee satisfaction survey or psychosocial risk analysis say about how motivating the work is?
— How do you monitor the energy sources of your employees?
— How do your employees get feedback? From the work itself or from you? And how often: daily, weekly, monthly or once a year?
— Do you let your employees switch between different tasks from time to time?
— Can they use their competencies and talents?

- Do they learn something every day?
- Do you give employees insight into the total picture?
- Do they have sufficient insight into how valuable and useful their job is?
- What decisions can employees make themselves?
- What do they need your approval for?
- Can you let go of control?

3.3 Motivating work should contain an acceptable amount of job demands

A job is not only characterized by positive, motivating features, but also has features that demand energy. These job demands or work requirements increase the risk of stress and burnout. Research shows that demanding aspects get in the way of satisfying the ABC. But not all demanding aspects are the same.

3.3.1 Stressors

Some requirements are true stressors. These obstacles eat up energy and get in the way of achieving your work goals. There are real "road blocks" that prevent you from doing your job well.

Requirements include:

- *Emotional demands*: Sometimes you are faced with issues that personally affect you or are emotionally demanding. Examples are nurses seeing others suffer or die, or teachers being seeing students being faced with extreme poverty or loneliness.
- *Physical demands*: Do you do light, medium, heavy or very heavy physical work? Garbage collectors walk miles per shift and lift heavy loads. Employees in a warehouse or butcher shop are active all day, sometimes in ice-cold, freezing conditions.
- *Role conflict*: Do you have to work on two projects at the same time? Do you have to deliver quality as well as finish quickly?

These tasks do not go together, making it difficult to choose. A chef hears from the waiters that the customers at a table are waiting too long. Does he still arrange the condiments nicely on the plate, or does he make sure that the less attractively dressed plates get to the table faster?

- *Role ambiguity*: Sometimes it is not really clear what you should do. As a salesperson, should you call your customers afterwards to ask if everything is okay? Or is that up to the customer care department?

- *Work-life imbalance*: You experience a work-life imbalance when you are so stressed or work such long hours that it is difficult to meet your obligations at home, meet up with friends or spend time on hobbies. The reverse is also possible: difficulties at home can haunt you at work.
  Finishing your work and taking care of your sick children at the same time, struggling with financial stress or working on your renovations? Such circumstances all cause more stress.

Stressors are detrimental to our ABC and are therefore a main cause of chronic stress, emotional exhaustion, and burnout. If you have a lot of stressors, you cannot concentrate very well. Those whose heads are filled with worries at home or doubts how to tackle tasks have less room to perform well. A little stress at work cannot hurt. But if this stress becomes chronic or too much to bear, we no longer have time to recover and recharge our batteries. Then it does become problematic.

CASE

In the public areas of a municipality, between the cleaning crew and the logistics staff, tensions often run high. The reason is that neither team know who is ultimately responsible for the content of the lockers. In principle, the cleaning crew is only allowed to clean the outside of the cabinets, while their contents belonged to the other team. But the logisticians felt that it was not they but the

---

cleaning team who should be sorting leaflets and gadgets. After a while, no one knew what exactly they were supposed to be doing.

"Everybody is a genius. But if you judge a fish by its ability to climb a tree, it will live its whole life believing that it is stupid."

ALBERT EINSTEIN

3.3.2 Challenges

Other demanding aspects of work are "challenges". Challenges require extra effort, but also offer learning opportunities and are motivating. For example, think about your last important deadline. Presumably, you pulled out all the stops to meet it and it gave you a lot of satisfaction and boosted your motivation.

- *Work and time pressure*: When you have to do a lot of things at once and/or you have to rush to get tasks done, we speak of work or time pressure. A domestic help who is only allowed to spend 2 hours per client instead of 4 hours has more work pressure, just like the journalist who has to hand in his articles at 6 p.m. sharp every day.
- *Cognitive demands*: When you have to remember a lot of things in your work or constantly have to stay focused, you experience cognitive demands. If an air traffic controller is momentarily distracted, it creates dangerous situations. Just like the pilot who has to put his plane on the ground during a snowstorm.

Challenges require energy, but they can also satisfy our ABC. Thus, it makes your job enthusing. A study in Scandinavia involving 160 self-employed people showed that work pressure was associated with more ABC. Self-employed people who experienced more stressors, on the other hand, felt less satisfied in their basic needs. Challenges are associated with more autonomous motivation, whereas stressors only diminish this autonomous motivation.

Usually, work is laced with various stressors and challenges. We too experienced work demands when writing this book. Our first book was a great adventure. We were under work and time pressure because we were writing the book parallel to our daily jobs and were facing a deadline. This sometimes resulted in less autonomy. We tackled a big, complex topic and therefore had to make difficult choices. Given the deadline, we could spend less time with family and friends than we really wanted to, resulting in less connection. Because we couldn't do everything at once, we sometimes felt less competent. And even though these stressors and challenges sometimes caused a lot of stress, they also gave us both a lot of energy and learning opportunities. The fantastic help from our publisher and support from the home front ensured that the real stressors remained within limits and our basic needs were more fulfilled than frustrated.

WHAT ABOUT YOU? HOW DO YOU EXPERIENCE JOB DEMANDS IN YOUR WORKPLACE?

— Do you have enough time to get your work done? Or do you have to rush constantly?
— Are there moments when you can concentrate 100% on your work or does a constant stream of emails and messages demand your attention non-stop?
— Do you take difficult situations that you experience at work with you for days on end?
— Do your back, shoulders, wrists or neck hurt when you come home at night? Do you have the proper lifting techniques? Do you have tools (e.g., a hoist, ergonomic chair) to make your work less physically demanding?
— Are there many unnecessary procedures or ambiguities?
— Can you go to your supervisor or colleagues if something is not clear?
— Do you sometimes have to do conflicting things?

- Can you keep work and home separated or do you prefer to let them intertwine?

What about you as a supervisor? What is the state of your employees' work demands?

- Do they experience too much cognitive or emotional strain in their job? Do you talk to them about this?
- Do they know what they have to do? Are their tasks clearly defined?
- Are they bored at work, or do you have too much work?

SUMMARY

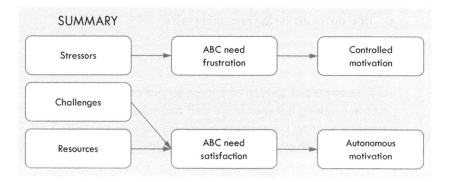

3.4 How to make jobs more ABC-proof

TIPS

The basic principles for making jobs more ABC-proof are simple:

- Increase the number of energy sources and challenges as much as possible.
- Limit the number of stressors to a minimum.

Be careful with the challenges, because on the one hand they can increase autonomous motivation. But if you have too many, they can cause stress. So look for a subtle balance.

3.4.1 Major adaptations

Markets change, new technologies make their appearance, and often there is a reorganization on the horizon. At times like this, major adjustments to a range of tasks may be needed. As a manager you play an important role here. The questions you can ask yourself then are:

1. What tasks should be taken up by the team?
2. How much time will each task take?
3. Who likes to do what task? Who gets energy from what?
4. For whom are these tasks real energy guzzlers?
5. How do we divide the remaining tasks?

CASE

In the commercial division of a large service company commotion is arising between office staff and sales staff. Due to market saturation, the company is focusing more and more on relationships with existing customers rather than on sales to new customers. As a result, sales employees are increasingly assigned customer care tasks. This is very much against the wishes of the employees who have spent years following up on the customer base. Suddenly, sales staff seemed to be running off with their customers. The resulting role conflicts and ambiguities caused frustration among the employees. And it undermined customer service. There was a need for more clarity. To solve the problem, discussions were held with both individual employees and the teams. What was each department supposed to do? How were the tasks distributed? In this way, clear job descriptions were formulated for the different functions within each department, together with the purpose, tasks, and expected results.

Employees could then indicate what they preferred to do and what made them feel more autonomous, belonging, and competent. A common support base was created for the new functions, and they were aligned across the different departments.

3.4.2 Small changes

Changes in the range of tasks do not always have to be accompanied by major organizational changes. Sometimes, small interventions in one or a few jobs are enough to give the autonomous motivation of your employees a boost.

What can you do as a manager to make jobs ABC-proof? Although executives do not always think about it, they have a great impact on the way jobs take shape. Executives with little experience or knowledge of job design often tend to strive for efficiency and are more likely to design jobs in a Taylorist manner. But it can also be differently, often even with minor interventions.

WHAT ABOUT YOU? WHAT DOES YOUR IDEAL JOB LOOK LIKE?

— What energy sources and challenges are you short of?
— What stressors do you want to reduce?

What about you as a manager?

— What can you do to improve the jobs within your team?
— As a manager, have you ever paid attention to your employees' job design?
— How did you try to improve their job design?

CASE

In one of the largest parcel companies, the ABC model runs like a thread through personnel policy. By asking staff how the distribution of the packages can best be organized, a lot of time is saved. The employees are given a great deal of say in the type of work they want to do. Those who like to get up early get an early round. Colleagues who prefer to start later do the evening shift. In this way, employees can adapt their working hours to their needs at home, they are satisfied in their ABC, and

---

> the work simply happens much faster and with more enthusiasm and less stress. It pays off! Parcel distribution is and remains a stressful job, but markedly few employees are absent and there is little stress or burnout. The number of accidents at work has also significantly reduced by listening to what employees have to say.

As an employee, what can you do yourself to make your job ABC-proof? Not only managers can adapt jobs. Employees themselves can take responsibility and make changes to their own job. They can do this through job crafting or negotiating i-deals.

A) *Job crafting*

"Job crafting" means that you adapt your job yourself as an employee. You continue to fulfill the same role, but adjust your tasks and relationships so that you have more energy sources, a manageable set of challenges, and fewer stressors. The goal is a better match between your job and your interests and capabilities. Job crafting helps you to find a job that you enjoy doing, that is fascinating and meaningful. This is very important because we spend a lot of time in and on our work.

> CASE
>
> The best-known example of job crafting probably comes from a study of cleaners in a university hospital. By talking to the cleaners, the researchers noticed that there were two types of cleaner. One type performed their job as it was described in the job requirements for cleaners: cleaning rooms, operating rooms, desks, and common areas was high on the agenda. The other type had a very different perspective on their job. They felt they were helping to support the patients' healing process and even called themselves "caregivers". They did a whole variety of tasks that were not in their job description at all. Some showed visitors the way, others regularly changed the paintings on the wards so that even intensive care patients could occasionally look at something new.

This example makes it clear that you can craft your job in three ways.

1) *Tasks*: You can customize your tasks. Either you do more (or less) (i.e. quantity) or you take on more (or less) responsibility (i.e. quality). For example, at the beginning of your job as an HR expert, you may like to focus on model development, though after a while you may prefer to share this information via lectures, in order to share your knowledge not only within the organization, but also outside it. Same job, different interpretation.

2) *Relationships*: You can also adjust/adapt the way you work together and communicate. Perhaps you sometimes ask advice from someone you look up to, strike up a cheerful conversation with the people on the cleaning crew, or recently commuted with that nice colleague from the other team. By meeting new contacts – even beyond those strictly necessary for your work, you enrich your job and you discover new opportunities.

3) *Perspective*: Finally, you can look at your job through different lenses. In this way you can find more meaning in your work. Keeping a roadside restaurant clean is then no longer about "cleaning", but about offering passers-by a comfortable stop. And cashiers will no longer simply scan products, but will make sure their customers pay the right price. It often helps to see your job as part of a bigger picture and thus to look for its task identity and task significance.

By adjusting your tasks, relationships, and your thinking about your work, you make changes to your energy sources, challenges, and stressors. For example, you can:

- take on additional tasks;
- learn new skills;
- educate yourself through online videos;
- phase out less pleasant projects;
- avoid that one colleague who causes you stress.

Job crafting offers many advantages, both for your employees and your organization. Through job crafting you can fulfill your ABC.

– The fact that you can adjust your job helps you feel more autonomous. You have control over your work and can focus on things you find valuable.
– The feeling that you belong to a group of colleagues also increases: you seek out more meaningful contacts.
– You will feel more competent in your job as you have designed it yourself.

Because you experience more ABC, you are more autonomously motivated, perform better, experience less stress, and solve problems even before they occur.

WHAT ABOUT YOU?

Have you already made adjustments to your work to be able to do it better and/or feel better about yourself?
- Have you ever taken on new tasks and passed on other tasks?
- Have you made sure that you have a little more variety in your job?
- Do you do things that are important to you?
- Can you finish tasks from A to Z?
- In the meantime, is it completely clear what you have to do? Are there no more contradictions? Have you ever looked at your job differently?
- What difference does it make to others?

And you as a manager?

Do you support your employees in the above-mentioned changes?

B) I-deals

In addition to crafting your work, you can also bet on i-deals or idiosyncratic deals: individual agreements that you negotiate with your supervisor. I-deals deviate from the standard and HR agreements that colleagues have, hence the term "idiosyncratic".

I-deals can be made about various aspects of your work:

- Your *flexibility*: are you allowed to work time- and place-independently? Maybe you can take time off on Wednesday afternoons if you're knocking off more hours on the other weekdays?
- Your *training*: are you very ambitious and do you want to grow in your job? Then perhaps you can follow additional training.
- Your *tasks*: if you like advising customers, you might be allowed to spend more time in the store instead of working the cash register.
- Your *terms of employment*: maybe you'd rather get an extra day off instead of a bonus?

Employees differ in which i-deal satisfies their ABC the most. Some fulfill their need for competence through an extensive master's degree, while others prefer to learn informally through peer review and challenging projects. Some prefer to work from the office to have their need for belongingness satisfied, while others prefer to work one or more days from home. In either case, i-deals are a great way to fulfill the ABC of each of your employees.

Like job crafting, i-deals are positive for both employees and the organization. Depending on the type of i-deal negotiated, they have a different effect. Flexibility i-deals improve work-home balance, whereas developmental i-deals primarily enhance performance. I-deals can also be positive for colleagues. Can you as an organization demonstrate that i-deals are also possible for them if they need them? That is very important.

CASE

Whereas Macy had always been a diligent and punctual domestic help, her manager noticed in recent months that his autonomous motivation was deteriorating. She showed up late for work, called in sick frequently, and her smile stiffened. Just last year, Macy had the feeling that she could continue to help her clients well. Now that was no longer possible: due to cutbacks she was given a maximum of two hours per client to iron, wash, go to the bathroom, run errands, and make lunch or dinner. Thus, she was under severe time pressure. Despite working hard, she could not give clients the care they needed. One day Macy stepped up to her manager. Together they came up with an i-deal, tailor-made solution. She would get especially those clients who went to the food bank. Processing the food required more time anyway and this way she could properly finish her tasks for those clients.

WHAT ABOUT YOU?

– Have you ever requested an i-deal from your supervisor or HR manager?
– Did you get it?
– What was this i-deal about?
– Did you know it was an i-deal?

What about you as a supervisor?

– Have you been asked for i-deals?
– Have you already allowed your employees to successfully negotiate i-deals?

But not everything that glitters is gold. Even though job crafting and negotiating i-deals are possibilities to improve your work and increase autonomous work motivation, their impact is not unlimited.

- Do you want sustainable and successful adjustments? Then make sure job crafting and i-deals are in line with the organization's goals and values. An educator may want to brighten up his job by gaming with the children. A lab technician might prefer to take a few shortcuts in the development of a vaccine. But such adaptations are not always in line with the values of the organization.
- Be considerate of your colleagues. Don't take nice tasks away from them and don't leave them with only unpleasant tasks. You can also work at the team level and explore new divisions of tasks together. In such an exercise everyone may first choose tasks they like. Then you divide the less pleasant work fairly. Does the statistician jump in the air when you indicate that you would rather not do any more analyses? Then you create a win-win. In addition, "everyone" must be given the chance to adjust and adapt their job. That way your job design become equitable, including those lower in the hierarchy, the less extrovert or the less proactive.
- Don't take on too much. Additional challenging projects can give a boost to your autonomous work motivation, but too much is indeed too much and you will soon feel controlled by the large amount of work.
- Taking on new tasks and responsibilities does not always mean getting paid more. This is why a colleague with those same responsibilities might get higher wages because they rolled into the job in a different way.

4. CAN COLLEAGUES AND CUSTOMERS ALSO BE MOTIVATING?

WHAT ABOUT YOU?

- Do you often work from home? If so, do you miss the contact with colleagues?
- When you are in the office, do you have much contact with colleagues?
- Do your colleagues help you?
- Do you have a good relationship with colleagues?
- Do you have a lot of social contacts at work? Do you have nice connections with customers, clients, vendors, or purchasers?
- Or do you experience more stress because of these contacts?

4.1 Social contact with colleagues

4.1.1 Three ways of providing support

The importance of social support from colleagues is widely recognized in the academic literature. Colleagues can provide support in three different ways:

First, people are social beings and the mere presence of others can be stimulating. Being able to work in a space where others are also present is motivating in itself. Students seek out each other's company and study together in the library, even if not a word is said. The mere presence of others also stimulates them to concentrate on their own work.

Consultants and writers look for a coffee bar where they can work undisturbed, but with some human murmurings in the background. And some employees like to go to the office so they can work with closed doors in the proximity to others.

Even the virtual presence of colleagues can count. For example, it is much more fun to work on an article or book together than alone, even when working from a distance. Once in a while you can email about your progress, and knowing that the other is also working on it gives your autonomous motivation a boost. Employees who work from home use instant messaging or texting in between to stay in touch with others. The presence of others does not always have to be physical.

CASE

Catherine works from home during the corona lockdown. At first she likes it: she no longer loses time commuting and she can work much more concentrated at home than in the office. But after a while, Catherine feels increasingly lonely. She only recently joined the company and does not yet know many colleagues. In addition, she is the only one with this particular job. She misses her colleagues. Catherine jokes about it during a Zoom call with one of her former classmates, "Maybe you guys should just turn on your video, so you can see each other. Or have a virtual coffee at 10 a.m." she says. Catherine takes on the advice and that extra bit of social contact with colleagues makes a world of difference to her.

Of course, it's not always pleasant or efficient to work together in the same space. Just think of landscape offices where calling colleagues (on the phone) are more disturbing than motivating background noise. And you may not be eager for a virtual coffee over small talk when you have an important deadline. If your other concerns are not taken into account, your need for autonomy becomes frustrated. So no real connection can develop. It only happens when there is mutual attention for each other's needs.

Second, colleagues offer *instrumental help*. Colleagues can help you with advice, practical support and information, or even by taking over your tasks for a while. "How do you do that again, combine cells in Excel?", "Who is responsible for accounting?", "How do you tackle such a report correctly?" Google knows everything, but colleagues often give much better advice, more in-depth and with a broader view of the context. Instrumental help from colleagues is not only fun, but also helps you to get the job done better or faster.

Third, colleagues also offer emotional help. The saying "Shared sorrow is half a sorrow. Shared joy is double joy" points to the importance of emotional help. Sharing your emotions with others is liberating: negative emotions are alleviated and positive emotions are strengthened. Just served an annoying customer? It's great to let off some steam with your boss! A project completed: a party with colleagues gives you double joy. A quotation that wasn't approved? Then we put chocolates on the table to ease the pain!

Of course, even with personal problems it can help to vent to colleagues. They may offer you a new perspective on your situation. A Monday morning chat about your weekend may offer added value if you can really build up a personal bond with your colleagues and expose yourself. When there is room to talk about, say, your difficult relationship with the boss, your divorce or problems with your children, you may experience real emotional support.

CASE

On a Monday morning, Karin, a mother of two adolescent children, makes an unpleasant discovery. She is about to leave for work and wants to take out the meat in preparation for dinner, but then discovers that one of her sons did not close the freezer. All the food is defrosted, and the entire storage room is flooded. When she arrives at work an hour late, she is still irritated, agitated, and angry. Colleagues notice immediately that something is wrong. It helps Karin to let off steam about it, because even though she considers work and private life to be separate worlds, this colors her mood, also at work. Her openness and the understanding of her colleagues means that after fifteen minutes, even she can laugh about it, and from that point, she can focus on work for the rest of the day.

"Success is not how high you have climbed, but how you make a positive difference to the world."

ROY T. BENNETT

4.1.2 Social support satisfies our ABC

Needless to say, social support from colleagues – in all its forms – is important. Research shows that it is one of the most important factors to be enthusiastic about your work, and the most important buffer for burnout in the face of high workloads, conflicts, and ambiguities. This is because social support plays an important role in satisfying our ABC.

Social support from colleagues is a strong source of connection. Reis and colleagues sought to find out which social activities most fulfilled our need for belongingness. They asked young people – for 14 days – to fill in, each time when their watches beeped, what they were doing and how strongly they felt connected to others at that moment. They found that real connections occurred especially when participants were able to talk together about something meaningful and felt understood and appreciated. Doing fun things together or just chatting also contributed, but deeper emotional support had the strongest effect.

Social support is also important for your needs of autonomy and competence. If you can go to others with your questions and concerns, without them judging, this also supports your need for autonomy.

Colleagues who, like you, occasionally nag about difficult assignments or a tough boss ensure that you feel less insecure about why things are not going smoothly for you. And when colleagues help you to do your work well, you learn and feel more competent.

The positive effect of social support is not limited to the person who receives it. Those who give social support also benefit. A study of Dutch police officers showed that officers who gave support, also became more enthusiastic about their work, especially when they gave that support during emotionally difficult times.

"Doing something for another gives more happiness than sitting alone in a spa."

DIRK DE WACHTER

But giving and receiving support is not always without risk. In the study of the police officers, positive effects were especially evident when the recipient of the support was open to it. It was important that they did not see it as a sign of weakness or an attack to their self-worth and personality. The colleague who always knows better may undermine rather than enhance your sense of competence. Then social support frustrates rather than satisfies your basic needs.

WHAT ABOUT YOU?

— Do you like to work with colleagues in one room? Are there agreements about when you can disturb each other and when you can work in a concentrated way?
— Do you dare to ask for support from your colleagues? Are you open to advice or do you see it more as criticism?
— Do you help your colleagues? When is your help welcome? When do colleagues not need it?

- Do colleagues dare to show their emotions at work?
- Can you confide in someone when you are having a hard time?
- When do you feel you have to "put on a faking mask" and act as if you are someone else?

And you as a manager?

- Do you force your employees to participate in social activities like the New Year's reception or digital coffee breaks?
- Do you have time to listen without prejudice to what your employees really care about?

4.1.3 Strengthening social support among colleagues

To ensure that colleagues can really help each other, good teamwork is necessary, in which they know each other well and can communicate with each other in an open way.

Then employees can:

- offer more social support to each other;
- better satisfy each other's needs;
- strengthen each other's autonomous motivation.

Connective communication

Connective or nonviolent communication focuses on empathy. In this way, you can connect with yourself and others. For this purpose, it offers a four-step model:

- perceive objectively;
- express your feelings;
- express your need that lies beneath;
- make a request.

There are quite a few similarities between SDT and nonviolent communication: both start from the Theory Y approach and emphasize the importance of needs and making a request, as opposed to a command or demand.

Both perspectives indicate that a command will quickly evoke resistance because it leads to controlled motivation. If you make a request, chances are that the other will respond to it, just because we like to help people. The needs of others also make ourselves happier.

CASE

From time-to-time, Steven needs help from his colleagues. He too helps colleagues at quieter moments and his requests are usually in balance with the help he provides. But the way Steven asked his colleagues for help irritates people. Statements such as: "Sofie, can you help me? I helped you last time" or "Come on, it'll get me done faster" don't always have the desired effect. After a training in nonviolent communication, Steven takes a different approach. He now states for example: "Sofie, there's a lot of work on the shelf again and I'm feeling rushed, insecure, and stressed. I just don't have enough time to help this client. Could you please give me a moment and check this PowerPoint?" Using this type of communication, Sofie feels she has the choice of responding favorably to the request or not and even though she sometimes has to disappoint Steven, the atmosphere improves by using nonviolent communication.

Supporting each other and communicating in a truly collaborative way are only possible when you really know each other. Is this possible in a work context? An intervention study shows it is!

Colleagues can learn to appreciate each other's positive sides and include and accept the darker sides, which benefits their ABC and thus their autonomous motivation. In this intervention study, Swedish bankers and real estate specialists got to know each other better in terms of character and behavior. After several sessions, the participants' autonomous motivation increased. In the control group, there was no such increase.

Other interventions can also help. Everything that contributes to real, authentic contacts, getting to know each other better, openness, attention, and empathic listening can be an asset. In this way you can offer and receive social support in a healthy way.

4.2 Social contact with customers, clients, students, or patients

4.2.1 Customer contact: a source of motivation?

Working with clients, customers, students, or patients can lead to difficult situations.

- Clients who yell or curse because they don't get what they expected: "I've never had such bad service."
- Students who come off as aggressive: "You're the worst teacher I've ever had."
- People who throw down the phone not too politely: "Leave me alone. I don't need anything."
- Clients who ask you questions you don't have the answers to: "Now I would have expected a little more help from you."

Such interactions and unsubtle negative feedback frustrate the ABC and do not at all contribute to anyone's autonomous motivation.

Fortunately, there is also a flip side to the coin and many also regularly receive positive feedback, such as:

- "Your service is fantastic."
- "You as a teacher have made a difference for my child."

- "Thank you for the pleasant conversation."
- "This is perfect, just how I wanted it."
- "Doctor, even though this is bad news, I am glad to hear it from you."

Customers, clients, students, or patients can also enhance the quality of the motivation of your employees. After all, service workers, teachers, healthcare providers and many others do work that elevates people. In fact, a great deal of work serves an end user.

- A nurse cares for patients.
- A construction worker helps build family homes.
- A researcher develops a drug to cure people.
- A receptionist helps new arrivals with directions.
- A chef prepares delicious meals for guests.
- An HR consultant brings teams and organizations to a higher level of functioning.
- An outplacement coach helps people find new jobs.
- Do you work for clients, whether inside or outside your organization?
- Do your patients or clients depend on your work?
- Do colleagues rely on you and your work to complete their tasks?
- Do you sometimes hear how you are making a difference in the lives of others?
- Do you get satisfaction from your work because it is valuable?

4.2.2 From "what" and "how" to "why": the motivating power of meaningful work

Being able and allowed to do something for others has a strong motivational power and makes us happy. It also provides you with a better understanding of and feel on the "why" of your work. Too often we focus on "what" we need to do and "how" it should be done. But this narrow focus on concrete tasks and procedures sometimes leads to employees losing sight of how they can contribute to the greater good. Sometimes they even forget how their work makes the lives of others better.

Being able to do something "important" or "valuable" is a weighty source of motivation. In the literature, being able to do something meaningful for others is also called "task significance" (see Part 2, Chapter 3) and it is an essential aspect of identification or "meaningfulness", as we discussed in Part 1: employees who identify with their work also see the value of their work. This is also called the human desire for benevolence, doing good to others, even if we don't know them.

Meta-analytic research shows that each of your basic needs is satisfied when you feel that your job contributes to or has an impact on the lives of others, whether inside or outside the organization.

CASE

For three years, Annie has been a grateful helper in Judy and Paul's chaotic family. Both have busy jobs, and they have four small children. The first time Annie arrived here, she didn't know where to start. The kitchen was exploding, laundry baskets were bulging, and there was a lot of vacuuming to be done. Yet every week, Annie began her day's work in good spirits. She could choose for herself what she started with, and she knew in advance that Judy and Paul would be very happy with everything she got rid of. Annie knows she has played a very important and significant role in that family, and if sometimes she has to work a little harder than usual, she is happy to do so.

Nadia is Johan and Richard's cleaning assistant. She has been employed for years for this moneyed, hard-working middle-aged couple who are childless. The house is full of valuable items that are completely dusted and shined twice a week. Nadia already

---

> expressed a few times that she was sorry that she couldn't make a bigger difference. Does everything really have to be dusted twice a week? She can, for example, also do the shopping or cook? Johan and Richard however insist that she needs spend her time cleaning, although Nadia doesn't find it very useful.

Paying extra attention to the "why of the work" and its "importance for others" is an important added value in jobs that, by their very nature, are not very intrinsically motivating. Adam Grant experienced this in the call center at his university.

In the American educational landscape, alumni with prestigious jobs are sometimes asked if they would like to donate money for a scholarship for brilliant but less fortunate students. These call centers are often staffed by students who also earn a little extra money this way. Few find it intrinsically motivating: on any day you are given a list of people to call according to a fixed protocol. More than once you get the lid on the nose. Trying to keep the call center employees' courage up, management has sought Grant's help.

Grant divided the employees into three groups. Before the intervention, the three groups performed equally well (or poorly). However, one month after the intervention, there was a marked difference. Employees from group 1 who had been allowed to really talk to the student and had experienced at first-hand how grateful s/he was, did much better than those from group 2, who only read a testimonial of the student, or employees from group 3, who did not have any contact with their beneficiaries. The employees from group 1 made significantly longer phone calls to potential donors and also raised more money.

Grant's research shows that seeing that your job adds value to others has a strong motivational impact. He focused especially on jobs that are naturally less intrinsically motivating such as those of call center workers and lifeguards in a swimming pool.

Lifeguards spend the vast majority of their time monitoring swimmers. Because they rarely get to do what they've been trained to do, namely saving lives, many rescuers find their job rather boring and far from autonomously motivating. Grant again had one group of rescuers read stories of other rescuers who had saved the lives of swimmers. The other group was given stories about how they could also use their knowledge and skills in everyday life. The results speak for themselves: rescuers who were allowed to see how important their work could be to others, after the intervention had a greater sense of impact, felt more appreciated, and found their work more meaningful. They subsequently worked more hours and helped others more than the rescuers in the group who were only made more aware of how they themselves could benefit from their work.

Of course, this way of motivating also works for those who find pleasure in their job. Regardless of whether or not a job is fun or engaging, by indicating how meaningful a job is, you increase autonomous motivation.

CASE

Henry works as a garbage collector. This allows him for example to start early so he can pick up his children from school in the afternoon. He also enjoys being on the job in the morning, before all the hustle and bustle, and doing physical work. His family sometimes looks down on this job, and people in traffic are not always friendly or patient. More than once, he has to duck out of the way of oncoming cyclists or reckless drivers.

People aren't always very considerate either: garbage bags are regularly far too heavy and residents call the head office angry when their trash is not emptied. The fact that their trash was not outside on time is something they often fail to mention. A Twitter action of one of the work students changes the atmosphere in the neighborhood. The student regularly posts how many miles he travels per day and how many tons of garbage they collect.

Gradually there are fewer complaints. Here and there, people even leave a word of thanks, and during warm weather some people even leave cool drinks. This really makes Henry feel good.

WHAT ABOUT YOU?

- What positive feedback have you received from clients or patients?
- Do you get little feedback from the people you work for? What can you do to get more feedback?
- Do you ever give compliments to service providers, such as your gardener or letter carrier, or do you merely stick to negative feedback?

"Our life is lost if we cannot live it in a meaningful way."

ERNST FERSTL

SUMMARY

Colleagues, patients, students, clients, and customers are not only a source of connection, they also help you feel more autonomous, belonging, and competent. It is nice to know that you are not alone and that you can mean something to others. Through their support and presence, they can help move our work forward.

Do you ever make time for a chat at the coffee machine or a shared lunch? Do you answer the question "How are you?" sincerely? Is there openness to your customers' perspective and story?

It doesn't always have to be grand initiatives. Connection and real contact are often found in small things.

5. MOTIVATING LEADERSHIP

- Do you have a good relationship with your employees?
- Can your employees come to you with all their questions? And with personal issues?
- Do your employees trust you?
- Do you have an eye for each individual employee?
- Do you address them on missed deadlines or errors?
- Do you check up on your employees? Do you think it is important that they do their work your way? And that they work enough hours each day?
- Are your employees allowed to make mistakes?

Note: If you are not a supervisor yourself, how would you evaluate your supervisor on the above questions?

5.1 The motivating power of classic leadership styles

5.1.1 Four leadership styles

Much ink has been spilled about how leaders can manage and motivate their employees. In the beginning, the focus was mainly on leaders' personality traits. But slowly it became clear that the behaviors that leaders exhibit are at least as important. Leaders are effective not because of who they "are", but by what they "do".

It is sometimes joked that there are as many leadership styles as there are leaders. The academic literature distinguishes between autocratic and democratic leaders, leaders who let their employees muddle along and those who keep a tight grip on the reins, transactional and transformational leaders, coaching, serving, and ethical leaders and so on.

A meta-analysis summarizing the existing literature on leadership divides these styles into four categories:

Passive leaders only take action only when problems get out of control	Relationship-oriented leaders give priority to relationships with their employees
– show little decisiveness; – postpone decisions; – ignore problems; – don't encourage their employees; – give little direction; – don't take initiative; – can be completely absent or unavailable to employees because of other meetings;	– pay particular attention to the people behind their employees and their emotions; – are concerned with their employees; – are open to their input; – are friendly, respectful, and accessible.
Task-oriented leaders **mainly focus on the tasks that** **employees perform**	**Change-oriented leaders** **lead employees through** **organizational changes**
– provide active leadership; – bring structure; – divide different roles among their employees; – set goals first; – anticipate problems; – define the quality requirements that the work must meet; – adjust the remuneration of the employees accordingly.	– mainly focus on changes within the work context; – guide their employees and team through turbulent times; – create a shared vision; – encourage their employees to innovate and to dare to take risks.

CASE

John has little ambition to be an executive, but he insists on becoming one to have a better chance of getting a long-awaited pay rise. John is convinced that as, an executive, he shouldn't interfere too much with what the team members do. After all, they know their tasks better than anyone else and have expertise in how they can best serve the customers. Anyways John is too busy to pay attention to such matters. He often locks himself up in his office. Emails from employees remain unanswered, especially if the questions are more complex. If, after multiple reminders, he finally provides a solution to a problem, his suggestion is often ad hoc.

Erik is just starting co-parenting after his divorce, and things sometimes go wrong with school hours and the children's hobbies. Fortunately, his boss Petra is very understanding and offers him the necessary flexibility to get used to the new situation. If Erik comes to the office 15 minutes late, he does not have to justify it. And if he needs to take care of something during working hours, she allows him to do so. Petra does make sure that the work gets done, but is a bit more flexible in her deadlines. She also inquires regularly how things are going, and Erik can go to her with his questions and concerns. That helps Erik tremendously during this difficult period.

It might seem good that John gives his team members a lot of freedom, but in fact he is more of a passive leader. He is often absent and only puts out fires when he has to, without a clear vision and without attention for all employees. Petra takes on her leadership in a more people-oriented way: she pays attention to the needs and concerns of Erik and empathizes with him.

"Understanding how to motivate organizational members is a critical component of effective leadership."

EDWARD DECI & RICHARD RYAN

Research shows that especially relationship- and change-oriented leaders fulfill the ABC of their employees and enhance their autonomous motivation. Such leaders, for example, adopt an empathetic attitude, focus on the needs of their employees, and allow their employees to grow. They guide employees through change processes by inspiring them to strive together toward a new ideal. They stimulate their employees to get to work themselves, taking into account their individual concerns. They act as role models by constantly aspiring to learn.

These leaders do not only deal with their employees in a supportive manner. In line with Theory Y, they also create the right context for high-quality motivation. Their employees experience fewer task demands and more sources of energy and, as a result, have more motivating jobs (see Part 2, Chapter 3).

WHAT ABOUT YOUR MANAGER?

— In which of the four categories would you place your supervisor?

  · Is he/she more of a passive leader?
  · Does he/she pay special attention to the people behind the employees?
  · Does he/she focus mainly on what needs to be done?
  · Does he/she accompany you toward a changing but desirable future?

— In what areas does your current supervisor do better/worse than previous supervisors?
— Is your supervisor available and directing you?
— Does he/she value you for good work?

Are you a supervisor?

— In what ways do you lead your employees?
— How do you manage your employees? How do you motivate them?
— Do you approach all employees in the same way?

5.2 ABC supportive leadership

5.2.1 What is ABC supportive leadership?

WHAT ABOUT YOU?

- Does your supervisor offer you choice and options?
- Do you feel understood by your supervisor?
- Can you communicate well and openly with your boss?
- Does he/she ensure that your work goals are clear?
- Do you trust each other?
- Is your opinion about your job important to your boss?
- Does your supervisor pay attention to your emotions?

Do you often answer "Yes" to the above questions? Then you have a leader who supports your ABC. SDT calls this autonomy or ABC supportive leadership. ABC supportive leadership was developed by SDT and is therefore additional to the more common ways of leading from the classic leadership literature we discussed above. It combines a relationship-oriented approach with a change-oriented approach. Such leaders know better than anyone how to respond to the ABC of their team members.

They increase the autonomy of their team members by:	They strengthen the belongingness of their team members by:	They satisfy the competence of their team members by:
– offering choices; – listening to their input; – Encouraging them to take initiative; – not using external rewards or punishments to steer behavior; provide a justification for why they make certain decisions or divide tasks, when choice and participation are not possible. They thus give a meaningful reason for their behavior, decisions, questions, and requests.	– showing genuine and authentic interest; – respecting and accepting them as they are; – taking into account their needs and emotions; – empathizing with their perspective; – not judging; – listening empathetically.	– strengthening their self-confidence; – helping them grow; – relying on their abilities; – focusing on their strengths; – seeing mistakes as learning opportunities; – focusing on their growth potential.

"Leaders who enable satisfaction of the three basic needs of ABC promote high-quality motivation where workers personally endorse and willingly participate in their work activities."

EDWARD DECI & RICHARD RYAN

As already discussed in Part 1, this ABC support leads to a set of positive consequences. This is reflected in the employees themselves, such as more positive emotions, better health, less stress, as well as in the organization, such as a lower turnover and less absenteeism.

Whether it is the direct supervisor, the one above him, the head of the department, or the CEO who works in ABC support, it makes no difference to the employees. In all situations, ABC supportive leadership creates positive impact. More than that, studies around the world come to the same positive results, both in more collectivist (e.g., China, Southern Europe) and in individualistic cultures (e.g., USA, Western Europe).

Ian is an executive at a large organization. He sees great added value in ABC supportive leadership by the direct managers and middle management. "The role of the leadership should not be underestimated when using ABC," he says. "When one can ensure an ideal environment, where personal opinion is solicited and respected and where employees at all levels experience connection and involvement, one will automatically achieve better results." For management, this means a major adjustment from years of tradition. Executives must first ask themselves: what is the state of their own ABC? What drives them in their job? By questioning themselves, managers can also better empathize with what it is like for employees to do this exercise.

5.2.3   Characteristics of ABC supportive leadership

A)   ABC supportive leadership is not controlling leadership.
ABC supportive leadership is diametrically opposed to controlling leadership. Controlling leaders frustrate the ABC of their employees and thereby increase their controlled motivation, which consists of internal and external pressure.

Controlling executives:

- are micromanagers: they try to meticulously manage their employees and impose all kinds of demands and expectations. Their demands have to do not only with the end result, but also with all possible intermediate steps. As a result, their employees hardly have the feeling that they can make their own choices;
- are authoritarian;
- require their employees to think and act in a certain way. This puts pressure on the employees' need for autonomy.
- behave at a distance, which frustrates the need for connection;
- often point out employees' mistakes or doubt their abilities. As a result, they undermine their need for competence;

- use punishments (e.g., withdrawing a promised promotion, threatening dismissal) and rewards (e.g., bonuses, premiums) to guide the behavior of their employees. They thereby increase the external pressure for their employees;
- introduce blame (e.g., "Because of your negligence we didn't win an order", or "Because you take long lunch breaks, the phone is unmanned for a long time and our customers have to wait longer") and shame ("Aren't you ashamed, you're the only one who always shows up late to meetings?"). They thereby provoke internal pressure in their employees.
- start from a Theory X perspective, believing their employees would rather be lazy than tired, are selfish and not to be trusted.

CASE

When Thomas is promoted to supervisor, he immediately rearranges the desks so that he can watch his subordinates' screens. In this way he ensures they will not be on Facebook or engage in other private matters during working hours. He also expects an update every week on what they have done.

Birgit is a real micromanager. She makes decisions over the heads of her people. But if one of her team members does the same in the opposite direction, everything has to pass through her. The atmosphere within the team is bad; mistakes are not tolerated. Team members work under heavy stress and there is no trust among them. After a while, no one dares to take any decisions. Every good idea is nipped in the bud and as soon as a decision is approved, Birgit presents it as if it is her idea.

WHAT ABOUT YOU?

- Do you delegate easily?
- Do you think your own way of working is the best and do you sometimes force or impose your way upon others?
- Do you easily let go of the work someone else is doing?

- Do you think your employees have sufficient knowledge to do their job?
- Are your employees in tune with what you think is important?
- Does it bother you when your employees look at their work in a different way?

What about your manager?

- To what extent does your supervisor want to control everything?
- Does he/she control what you do and think?
- Does he/she think you are withholding information?

Employees will do what a controlling supervisor demands. But they don't do so wholeheartedly. Often, therefore, they only do what is expected of them half-heartedly. And the stress associated with this controlled motivation also makes them more susceptible to burnout.

CASE

Ella wants Youssef to contact customer X for a long time. She hopes that he will place a large order before the end of the year. Youssef says he will get on it, but he never does. After a while, Ella loses her patience. "Youssef, I want you to contact the client before the end of the week or this neglect will be part of your evaluation file. You are refusing to include potentially great customers." Youssef is tired of Ella's whining and wants to avoid a negative evaluation, so he decides to contact the customer. The conversation goes reasonably well, but Youssef does not enjoy it and is reluctant to follow up on the customer's requests. The contact is diluted again. In the end, Ella doesn't reach her goal to bring in a major customer, as she has put too much pressure.

Rather than putting so much pressure Ella should have looked for the reason of Youssef's resistance. What made Youssef unable to motivate himself to prepare for the interview and make contact?

What needs were being frustrated here? Ella could have used this resistance to see what, according to Youssef, was going wrong in his work or in the department, in order to improve how things worked. And even though she may not have been able to solve all of Youssef's problems, the attention to his needs would have set a beautiful process in motion. But what did Ella do? Instead of reversing the resistance, she created even more pressure, and soon Youssef botched the task to get rid of this compulsion.

B) *ABC supportive leadership does provide structure*

Is ABC supportive leadership a "soft" way of leading? Are ABC supportive leaders not concerned with the tasks or job content of their employees? Do they dare not impose deadlines, give negative feedback, be critical or follow up on the quality of the work?

Definitely not! ABC supportive leadership is not "laissez-faire" or passive leadership. Ideally, a leader combines a focus on relationships and change and gives attention to the tasks at hand, so that everything stays in balance.

According to SDT, the best leaders combine ABC support with structure, such that they:

- structure tasks well;
- set clear expectations;
- follow up on performance;
- provide clear and encouraging feedback.

This leads to the satisfaction of the need for competence and autonomous motivation. Too little structure creates chaos. Too much structure can appear controlling.

CASE

Peter learned in a leadership course that autonomous teams were the future. Inspired by the course, he instructs his team to take care of

---

> their own leave arrangements from now on. Because the entire team consisted of young parents, everyone wants the same schedules and the same weeks of holidays during summer. So it all goes wrong. Peter just "let go". He offers no structure, no interpretation, he just gives the assignment, without guidance or input.

Peter's case is a good example of laissez-faire leadership. With real ABC support, Peter would clearly provide structure in a first meeting: "Which leave times are popular? How do we best distribute them? What is each team member's first choice? Which days come second?" Only then the puzzle can begin. "Who gets their first choice? Who is also happy with their second choice? Who gets their preference next year?" Meeting after meeting, an ABC supporting executive would hand over the transfer responsibility for the process to his employees. Step by step, they would learn to support each other's ABC.

There are however some pitfalls to take into consideration.

Pitfall 1: "I have to check, otherwise nothing will happen." Sometimes supervisors feel that they do "have to" monitor and control their employees. "If I don't check on them, they won't be on time," or "If at the end of the day I don't ask how many shelves they filled, they'll do less than expected." That idea starts from Theory X and the assumption that employees would rather be lazy than tired. In Part 1, we saw that your "thinking" also determines your "doing". Those who assume that their employees are lazy will control them and thus destroy their autonomous motivation.

Pitfall 2: "I don't dare to follow up. Suppose they find me controlling." Out of fear of appearing controlling, some executives are afraid to follow up on their employees: "They might think I'm controlling them".
So they're afraid to ask them why they didn't meet a deadline, why they're always late, or why there were so many mistakes in that report.

But monitoring and following up are not the same thing. Not "monitoring" doesn't mean that you don't follow up on the work of your employees, colleagues or coworkers. If you don't follow up, then you make them feel you don't care and their work doesn't actually matter. "No one cares whether or not I do my work well or deliver on time... Nobody cares." Thus, by not following up on your employees, you undermine their need for belongingness and competence, and cause them to perceive their job as less meaningful. Follow-up doesn't mean you're continuously controlling their behavior, but that you're interested in their work. You are concerned with what they have done, and in what way. By following up, you pay attention and show you are "present", that their work is meaningful and that you will support them if needed.

WHAT ABOUT YOU?

— Do you sometimes worry that your coworkers will find you too controlling?
— Are you afraid to ask why someone keeps making so many mistakes?
— Do you address your employees when they don't do something right?
— Do you show interest in their work?
— Do you sometimes feel that nothing you say or ask has an impact? And that the only way to motivate your employees is through external pressure? "That's the way to do it."
— Do you dare to be ABC supportive?

5.2.4 How can a manager become more ABC supportive?

As described above, there are many benefits to ABC supportive leadership. A crucial question then is: is it possible for everyone to become ABC supportive? Can everyone do it? Can you? Yes, with some training, it certainly is possible. Intervention studies show that leaders can learn through training to become more ABC supportive.

Deci and Ryan, along with their colleagues, indicated as early as 1989 that executives could be trained to be more ABC supportive. The company where the training took place was going through a difficult period: strong competition was causing a serious decline in sales and profits. By focusing on ABC supportive leadership and the ABC of the employees, the company hoped to turn the tide. During the training, an external consultant guided all executives, from top to bottom.

During this intervention:

- executives learned to let their employees take more initiative, let them make their own choices and pay attention to issues that the employees found most relevant;
- the importance of informal constructive feedback was emphasized. There was a "negative feedback" or "mistake-oriented" culture in the organization. Even compliments were given in a controlling rather than supportive manner (see Part 2, Chapter 2) and therefore had a demotivating effect;
- managers were trained to see their employees' perspective more, to really listen to them and to pay attention to their needs, frustrations, and emotions.

Thanks to this intervention, managers grew in their ABC support. This also had a positive effect on the employees. They gained more confidence in the organization and management, even when they barely had any contact with senior managers.

"A leading contemporary theory of motivation can provide leaders with an evidence-based framework for how to effectively motivate workers."

EDWARD DECI & RICHARD RYAN

Other intervention studies also confirm that ABC supportive leadership can be learned. In a residential psychiatric hospital for adolescents, management decided to focus not only on the ABC of the managers but also on that of the patients. Through ABC workshops, employees' autonomous work motivation, satisfaction, and well-being all went up. What's more, it made employees less controlling so that the ABC of the youngsters was also more fulfilled, and their autonomous motivation for their treatment increased. Not only employees, but also patients, clients, and customers benefit from training that responds to the fulfillment of the ABC.

TIPS

— Be patient. Be aware that this won't all work out by snapping your fingers. If, as a boss, you have never listened to your employees and suddenly decide to give them a say, it will come as a surprise to them and may take them a while to adapt to your changed behavior.
— Get on board with it, too. If your employees give you input, take this into consideration. For example, Hannah kept asking for input from her team members, but as soon as it came, she completely ignored it and pushed her own vision.

"As a manager, you will not be motivating your employees, but create those circumstances in which they will optimally motivate themselves."

EDWARD DECI & RICHARD RYAN

CASE

The senior team leaders of a medium-sized company want to become more ABC supportive. During several workshops, the managers learn more about SDT and during the workshops and training that followed, they are given the tools to motivate team leaders in their daily tasks. By using an ABC supportive approach, the SDT consultant is able to slowly make the executives feel what they can achieve if they put more effort into their employees' ABC. Executives feel free to express their questions and complaints and the consultant lets them come up with their own solutions, which makes it even more interesting for everyone. The passion and enthusiasm with which the workshops are conducted give all participants a boost of confidence. A real boost for all managers and their teams.

5.2.5 Preconditions for ABC supportive leadership

A)   Without trust there is no ABC supportive leadership
ABC supportive leadership clearly departs from Theory Y: as a manager, you trust your employees and believe that they have your and the organization's best interests at heart. This does not mean there should be blind trust. It does mean that everyone is entitled to a fair chance. An ABC supporting manager then tests whether and how adjustment is needed.

There is an interesting dynamic at play between control and trust: the more you trust someone, the less control you need. You will only control if you don't trust your employees. If your employee says that she can concentrate better at home, and you trust her, you won't find it necessary to call her during the day or ask her after a workday what she has been doing. If the results still fail, then follow up with an honest non-judgmental conversation about where things are going wrong. If a site manager trusts his team to put on their safety helmets and shoes, he will not install cameras on the job sites.

What does it mean to trust someone? Trust consists of three parts. You trust someone if you think they:

- can do it (competence);
- are loyal (concerned with your interests and those of the organization);
- have integrity (honesty, consistency).

Melissa is allowed to work from home two days a week because her boss Tom trusts her to do it (competence) and believes she cares about the organization's interests and will therefore not only take care of her home (loyalty) but also correctly reflect all that she has done (integrity). Now assume that Tom does not trust Melissa, then he can indicate why he does not trust her. "Melissa, I know you are loyal and have integrity, but I doubt your abilities in this. I've noticed that you are often distracted even at the office, so I wonder how this will go when you work from home. Would a training course for time management help you to deal with this?"

"If you have confidence, you do not have to see the whole staircase to take the first step."

MARTIN LUTHER KING

B) Psychological safety as cause and effect

Psychological safety refers to an interpersonal climate in which you feel that you can speak freely in your team or to your boss. And this without losing face, being seen as incompetent or being embarrassed. That's not an easy thing to do. If you have doubts about doing the right thing and act correctly, or you have reservations about how your colleagues or boss deal with things, you are not inclined to bring that up spontaneously. There is a lot at stake: the collaboration, the perception of your expertise, and your ego.

Sometimes successful teams seem to make more mistakes compared to less successful teams, but research shows this is not the case. It's just that they talk more about their mistakes instead of keeping quiet. Moreover, there is no hesitation in admitting mistakes. For example, Steve Jobs has been credited with the story of an Apple employee whose mistake had just lost the company

$400,000. So Jobs invited this person to come and speak with him. Not because he wanted to fire him for failure but because his attitude was: "We just invested $400k in a learning experience, that is why I want to hear about it!"

You will only really succeed in motivating your employees autonomously, through their ABC, if the work environment is psychologically safe. Only then you can let go, trust, communicate openly and learn from mistakes. Then employees also dare to share their perspective and dare to be honest about their emotions. The higher up in the organization, the more difficult that sometimes becomes.

"Anyone who has never made a mistake has never tried anything new."

ALBERT EINSTEIN

C) *The broader organizational climate also plays a role*
The effects of ABC supportive executives are not always positive. For example, when employees felt uncertain about the continuation of their jobs, Deci and Ryan noticed a much smaller positive effect. They therefore caution that the effects of autonomy-supportive leadership also depend on the broader climate in the organization.

Do all executives, from line managers to the CEO, commit to the ABC? Are all HR practices focused on meeting basic needs? An organizational climate in which the ABC and the autonomous motivation of employees are central pays attention to:

- autonomy and free will;
- cooperation, and the feeling that each employee has an important role in their team;
- personal progress and development of competencies and skills.

An ABC supportive climate avoids:

- pressure on employees;
- focus on rewards;
- rivalry and competition among employees;
- comparing their skills (who performs best?);
- a single-minded focus on the outcomes of a task;
- seeking public recognition and approval from your colleagues and boss.

When everyone speaks the ABC language, it simplifies communication and increases the likelihood of success.

5.3 The importance of communication: the ABC language

- How often do you say something "has to" be done?
  Or do you use the word "must"?
- How often do you give orders?
- When you ask something of others, do you express it
  as a request or a demand? Can they say "No"?
- Do you find it rude or annoying when others say no?
- Do you think about what others like or find
  meaningful about the task that you would like to delegate?

Communication plays an important role if you want to motivate others. Actually, you can communicate in two ways. Inviting and connecting versus coercive and controlling. You can use this communication in your verbal interactions, but also in emails, newsletters, websites, and even chat messages.

Inviting and connecting language is characterized by:	Coercive and controlling language is characterized by:
– open questions: "Could you…?", "Will you please…"; – choice : "You can consider …"; – open verbs, such as want, try, propose: "I suggest you do this, would you like that?"; – check: "Do you like this?", "What do you need?"; – encourage: "You can do this", "You will do this well", "I trust you in this"; – invite: "I invite you to try it this way"; – informational (non-compulsory) tips: "Maybe you can try it this way"; – consultation: "Which deadline is feasible for you and okay for the customer?", "How would you approach this?"	– commands: "Now finish this project asap!"; – must statements: "You must …"; – "It's the way it should be", "because I say so"; – controlling language: "Can you finally do it the way I expect you to?", "I expect you to do it this way"; – conditional positive feedback: "Good, this is just what I expected from you"; – self-esteem-related statements: "Someone with your profile should be able to do this"; "I expect more from someone with your education"; – guilt induction: "I and the entire management team are deeply disappointed in…"; – shame: "Aren't you ashamed of your mistakes?"

From the perspective of SDT it is best to avoid controlling language and to use inviting, connecting communication such as put forward by Marshall B. Rosenberg as much as possible. He advises to talk without judgments and always start from your own needs.

It is therefore important to first gain insight into your own need satisfaction: any unmet needs that make you angry, sad, or anxious and any fulfilled need that makes you hopeful, happy, and energetic. If you can formulate a clear request based on your own needs, it will be easier for the other to fulfill your needs.

"Every criticism, judgment, diagnosis, and expression of anger is the tragic expression of an unmet need."

MARSHALL B. ROSENBERG

In doing so, however, it is important that you are open to the other's no. Know that every "No" is a "Yes" to something else.

- "Demanding" increases the other's sense of pressure and coercion. People do not like to be pressured. They want to get into something themselves, autonomously and voluntarily.
- "Requesting" gives others the opportunity to help you. By expressing your need, you show that what you are asking for is very important to you. In this way you can motivate the other (autonomously) to respond to it. This altruistic behavior fulfills their ABC: they choose to help someone, feel connected to the person they are helping, and feel competent because of this.

In addition to your own needs, the needs of your coworkers, supervisors, and colleagues are also important. A simple tool to get in touch with the needs of others is not to speak, but to listen empathically. This enables you to see the other as an individual with their own perspective, wishes, and desires. By really listening, without judging, you can truly connect with this person and strengthen your mutual need for connection.

The objective of Nonviolent Communication is not to change people and their behavior in order to get our way: it is to establish relationships based on honesty and empathy, which will eventually fulfill everyone's needs."

MARSHALL B. ROSENBERG

CASE

Dirk turns his marketing company over to Bo and Guy, but continued to work there on a freelance basis and kept his office on the first floor. Upon his hiring, Akim is given one of the desks on the ground floor. He however misses the contact and direct communication with colleagues, who are one floor up, next to

Dirk. "Maybe they could switch desks?" Bo suggests to Dirk. Even though he is a case manager for years from that desk, and relinquishing this spot is not easy, Dirk agrees. He agrees to move by March. But nothing happens. Bo questions Dirk about this, and again he says that he will move, but in May he is still there. In a training course on ABC focused communication, Bo learns more about SDT and the ABC language. Through role-playing, Bo learns to empathize with the emotions and needs of herself and Dirk. Inspired by her new insights, Bo starts a new conversation with Dirk. "Dirk, what's stopping you from moving?" She also assesses the extent to which Dirk's needs are met or frustrated. His need for autonomy is fine, but he feels frustrated in his needs for belongingness and competence. He fears he will lose connection when he is one floor down and wonders whether — after all these years — he still can contribute enough. The whole conversation feels like an "aha-moment" to both of them and shortly thereafter, Dirk and Akim switch desks.

Connecting communication is the opposite of coercive language that is based on judgments, interpretations, and reproaches: "Because you are not communicating sufficiently, I'm angry and don't feel good about my job." Connecting communication starts from your own needs: "I feel insecure about the restructuring. Can you give me a little more clarity on this?"

Coercive language evokes resistance. People do not like to be pressured or controlled. Sometimes people are willing to do something, but because you address them in a coercive way, they experience more stress, withdraw or just wipe their feet on the task.

"Knowledge speaks, but wisdom listens."

JIMI HENDRIX

"Most of us grew up speaking a language that encourages us to label, compare, demand, and pronounce judgments rather than to be aware of what we are feeling and needing."

MARSHALL B. ROSENBERG

You can also provide clear structure and direction through inviting language. In the longer term, this leads to better results, especially if you expect quality work motivation. Being ABC supportive also helps to better understand the underlying motives behind the behavior better. Why is there resistance? Don't assume that resistance is negative, but view it as a source of information. People who don't follow the rules are not necessarily disobedient. There may be other issues at play.

CASE

During the corona pandemic a group of workers in an automotive company are at the check out every afternoon at 4 p.m. They do not take into account the requested physical distance of 2 meters. They have already been asked several times to keep their distance. This first appears friendly, then just polite, but after a while demanding. Nothing works. The last mail was very forcefully worded. This increases the dissatisfaction among the workers. But still they stand equally close to each other at the check out. So what is going on here? Very simple. The group of people is too large, so some at the end of the line have to wait up to up to 20 minutes before they can tap out. To solve this issue, a structural solution is needed. Now, Group A is allowed to tap out at 10 to 4, group B at 4:00, and so on. The workers did not intend to violate the rules but the existing structures simply did not allow for compliant distance keeping.

5.4 ABC support in difficult times: organizational change and work from home

Executives today face many challenges: organizations are constantly changing and, in the meantime, working from home has become a must. How do you motivate employees for this organizational change? And how do you motivate them from a distance? Here, too, ABC supportive leadership helps to face resistance toward the change and to stimulate the connection and involvement of employees, even if they work from home.

"With every choice you make, be conscious of what need it serves."

MARSHALL B. ROSENBERG

CASE

The middle management of a large pharmaceutical company is tasked with introducing a new way of working. For most employees, this means a drastic change in their way of working, which causes resistance. The executives are unsure how best to go about it and wonder to what extent the basic principles of SDT can help and go and talk to their employees. In the first instance the managers are looking for the causes of the resistance. It is about fear of the unknown, distrust, fear of what one may lose, uncertainty, no control, and the desire to maintain the status quo. They get all this information by listening to their employees with empathy and full attention. The employees feel better understood as a result, which increases their sense of connection. The managers also acknowledge the employees' feelings. In this way, they built mutual trust. This change is accompanied by uncertainty, fear, frustration, anger, and even sadness. In addition, the management explains why the transformation is necessary. What is the added value? By formulating the change very concretely, fear and uncertainty decreases. In the final implementation phase, they involve the employees to the maximum. This also increases their involvement and volition (autonomy). Because they themselves also get more grip on the transformation and their work situation, their sense of competence increases.

WHAT ABOUT YOU?

Do you sometimes have trouble getting people on board and motivating them for a change?
When does it work? When does it does not work? Is it the change itself or the way it was communicated?

Getting your employees to work from home and at the same time motivating them is an important but not always obvious challenge. From an SDT point of view it doesn't really matter whether employees work in the office or remotely. Their autonomous work motivation depends on the degree to which their ABC is fulfilled, not their work location.

- Is there autonomy? Find a good balance between sufficient supervision and structure, to avoid chaos without having too much control. You want to offer sufficient autonomy: give employees the space to choose their own hours and the order of tasks. But also offer structure by monitoring performance and ensuring the quality of their work.

- Do employees feel connected? Connection is the hardest need to address while working remotely. Physical isolation and the absence of nonverbal support can lead to loneliness. Support meaningful "connections" and communication with, and among, team members:
- either individually through regular contact (e.g., email, phone, video calls); or
- at the group level by developing an online community.

Here, try to find a good balance between, on the one hand, time for the team to create connection, and on the other, the individual needs for autonomy.

- Is there enough competence? Can everyone easily handle the necessary tasks? Do they have all the tools to do their job? A suitable space? Do they know who to contact in case of problems?

TIPS

How can you promote the ABC of your employees through ABC supportive leadership?

Autonomy	Belongingness	Competence
– Avoid any kind of pressure and coercion, but do follow up. – Stay away from any form of micromanagement, even when employees are working remotely. – Design meaningful and interesting tasks. – Provide enough variety and challenges. – Make sure your employees experience "control" over their tasks and decisions. – Let your employees choose for themselves as much as possible. – Let them make their own decisions. – Let them participate in decision-making. – Avoid rewards and recognition that come across as controlling. – Find out where resistance comes from: "Every no is a yes for something else." – Explore different options. Don't get stuck on one solution.	– Be empathetic. – Listen openly and attentively. – Explore the concerns and needs of your employees. – Demonstrate that you understand their position. – Don't judge or accuse. – Offer different communication channels when employees are working work on location: Zoom, Skype, telephone… – Make time for a conversation, even when employees work from home. – Ensure a good team spirit. – Have attention for individual needs. Follow up on feelings of loneliness with increased interaction such as a daily phone call.	– Help your employees develop their goals. Are they realistic? – Provide accurate feedback. – Avoid competition. – Give everyone an equal opportunity. – Evaluate each individual based on their progress, creativity, and effort. – Give employees time and space to develop their skills. – Give home-based employees structure: within what time frame do you expect them to work? Take into account their private situation. – Set your own boundaries: "No, I am not available the whole weekend." – Also give feedback from a distance. Agree on the best way to do so. Do you put your comments directly into their reports? Or do they prefer to get them by email or via a Zoom meeting? – Follow up on their performance.

Conclusion

We hope that after reading this book, we have convinced you of the value and importance of high quality, autonomous motivation and satisfying (rather than frustrating) the basic psychological ABC-needs for Autonomy, Belongingness and Competence. When you are able to find these at work (or any other life domain for that matter), you can rest assured that you and others around you will function optimally: have high levels of energy and mental well-being, develop positive attitudes towards work and the company you're working at and perform the best you can. You yourself can take action to find your high quality, autonomous motivation and satisfaction of your ABC needs. But you are most likely to be optimally motivated when you can work in an environment where pay is sufficient and is not top of mind day in day out, when your job includes a lot of job resources and few demands and when you can find others, including your manager or supervisor who understands ABC-support. We hope you can work in such an environment and you can create such an environment for others. Good luck!

Annex: THE ECONOMICS OF MOTIVATION

- How does your organization invest in employee motivation?
- How would you convince your CEO to invest in motivating your employees? Which language do you need to speak?
- What is the return on investments of your motivational programs such as training, talent management, or career development?

CFO: "What if we invest in our people and they leave?",
CEO: "What if we don't and they stay?"

---

1. The importance of investing in people

The economy goes up and down in cycles, with periods of full employment and low levels of unemployment on the one hand, and times when a downturn increases unemployment, on the other. But regardless of what cycle a business finds itself in, in today's organizations it's the people who create value, with their effort, talent, knowledge, training, competencies, relationships, capabilities, strengths, and so on. People create value. Hence, we need to invest in them. The question is how economic benefits can be quantified and related to cost in order to arrive at a profitability ratio.

CASE

Frank is an HR director at a large European telecom company. He has submitted a proposal to the Executive Committee (ExCom) for investing in a talent management program introducing the ABC framework into one of their strategic business units. Total cost over the next two years: $1.2m. Frank's proposal is competing

---

for budget against other projects such as investments in software, marketing, and infrastructure. After his pitch, the CFO turns to Frank who is standing in front of the entire ExCom. "What is the expected return on investment of the ABC talent management program?" he wants to know.

Frank responds by pointing at better motivation leading to increased employee engagement, better communication, higher levels of creativity and innovation, lower absenteeism, and reduced employee turnover. "That all sounds great and I believe you. But I need numbers such as ROI or payback from you so that I can evaluate your program in economic terms and compare your proposal to other projects." Frank knows his project has huge potential but has a hard time translating it into "dollars and cents"; he wonders how to do this.

High-quality, autonomous motivation is efficient to promote both performance and well-being at work. But we could also state that we need to stimulate high-quality motivation before the employment period in order to increase the likelihood that it will lead to higher performance and more retention later on. This trio is called recruit, enable, retain.

Take selection, for example. Companies usually have some numbers on the selection process: how much did publicity cost, what salary is offered, how many applications were received, how many candidates fit the bill, how many interviews were conducted, how many stayed within the organization the first year, etc. Even though organizations may have these numbers, companies usually don't have a method to calculate the most cost-efficient method.

"You don't build a business. You invest in people and then the people build the business for you."

(unknown)

The acronym VUCA – volatile, uncertain, complex, ambiguous – is often used to describe today's workplace. Everything changes rapidly, with unexpected turns and it may sometimes be hard to make sense of it. The good news is that numbers cut through all that like a hot knife through butter.

That is why consultants who sell machinery, software, hardware, and equipment usually use return on investment (ROI) as a measure to promote their products; because it is easy to manage. But while inanimate things are easy to manage, there also is little potential to differentiate yourself from the competition. That is why people represent the most important source of competitive advantage. Only people can bring high-value differentiation, be it in the way they collaborate, how they identify new solutions and products, or how they help overcome challenges.

You cannot motivate people directly, but only through creating a work environmental under which ABC is satisfied. Stated in monetary terms, companies need to invest in high-quality work environments for employee motivation. In this chapter, we will make the invisible... visible. The intangibles of high-quality work motivation will be translated into monetary terms.

2.   Focus both on fixing what is broken and nurturing what has potential to grow

In research, it is sometimes said that "bad is stronger than good", meaning that the negative more easily catches our attention than the positive. Translated into needs, this means that frustrated needs immediately capture our attention, so that the problem, trouble, or emergency is more quickly solved. This process is instantaneous and rapid. This also means we are less inclined to have a look at the positive side, at need satisfaction. Even though it is as important as looking at the negative, it simply appears less immediate and pressing to have a look at positive than at negative needs.

The 4 Ds at work

This mechanism has implications for the work setting: We are more inclined to address the "4 Ds":

- Damage
- Disorder
- Disease
- Dysfunction

In other words, our attention is caught when a worker sabotages equipment, behaves illegally, is absent due to sickness, or is creating problems in a unit. These obvious problems immediately catch our attention and we tackle them. Thank goodness.

The same applies to "soft" issues such as psychological harassment, high psychosocial risks, and short- and long-term insurance disabilities claims. These issues, if not tackled, cost money (we can have a specific cost or value for it) and can create even more drastic problems; hence we address them.

While there is a cost on the "negative" side (for example when an employee is on long-term sick leave), there is also a "positive" side of the story. Positively engaged employees, for example, can create more value than (actively) disengaged employees. In other words, we can put a dollar sign on the negative and the positive sides of employee work motivation. There is a need to communicate (or translate) motivation in the language of business – ROI, payback, or "money" in general.

3. SDT and ROI

For all this, there is a solution in that SDT has developed approaches to quantify the quality of work motivation in money terms, and hence put ROI numbers on investments in employees.

We can put a dollar sign on the circumstances we put in place so that people flourish, thrive, and perform. Stated differently, so that people can create real value for an organization.

SDT has tools to calculate and communicate motivation in numbers, and:

- ROI numbers are surprisingly high.
- Numbers confirm: people are not only a source of sustainable competitive advantage, they may well be the best investment for companies.
- We need to "put our money where our mouth is".
- Tools exist, there is no excuse not to use them.
- Organizations need to apply these numbers.

"Worldwide, and in organizations of every type, people processes' are failing to keep pace with a changing business landscape [as] the lack of being able to talk the business language of ROI prevents (executive) buy-in."

(from "The State of Human Capital 2012: The False Summit, McKinsey & Company and The Conference Board")

An application of the Economic Value Added (EVA) model

Let's have a look at the Economic Value Added (EVA) model in real life. This will help portray how SDT research and intervention results, when translated in monetary terms, can be communicated more impactfully.

CASE

Thomas, a management consultant, is meeting the CEO of a large multinational company to pitch the importance of investing in people as a source of sustainable competitive advantage. "People feel, therefore they perform", he lectured the CEO. Thomas proposes an intervention project to increase employee engagement. Estimated project cost: around $350,000. The CEO responds: "This all sounds very interesting, but you need to show me the money! What is the project ROI so that I can sell this to my Executive Committee?" Thomas used the ABC-based EVA model — Economic Value Added — for a cost-benefit analysis of people investments to produce an ROI figure for the CEO.

In today's knowledge economy, companies need to invest in organizational design, training, and development to recruit, retain, and enable employees to bring out the best in their workforce. Such investments need to follow executive decision-making processes. Therefore, people investment projects require financial analysis to be expressed in cost-benefit terms, the "language of business". The return on investment (ROI) of people investment projects can then be compared to other corporate investment proposals by corporate decision-makers such as the Executive Committee and Board of Directors. Until recently, people investments were suffering from a communication dilemma. That is, people investment project proposals did not speak the "language of business" due to the lack of an economic model allowing for cost-benefit analysis.

EVA was developed in practice as part of an original, academic ABC research project. The model can be applied to all facets of people investments at work. By providing projected and actual ROIs, EVA enables informed, executive decision-making based on sound academic credentials. Since publication of the original academic research report in 2019, the model has been applied in corporate settings in countries such as Sweden, the U.S., Germany, Australia, and Luxembourg. Actual project ROIs suggest, that, in a knowledge economy, investments in people may well be the most profitable corporate investments, both from a qualitative and financial point of view. The following case study based on

Thomas' consulting project introduces the EVA framework using a five-step process.

Consider SmartCo, a company with 200 employees who on average earn $50,000 a year. An initial survey showed that 40 employees were "engaged", 140 "disengaged", and 20 "actively disengaged", with an average engagement score of 4.1. The correlation between the ABC of autonomy, belongingness, and competence (all three added together to an ABC score) and engagement was 0.5. That is, if employees' ABC scores increase by 10%, their engagement can be projected to increase by 0.5 x 10% = 5%. Thomas' project design included a 12-month intervention in a Time1/Time2 pre/post design to increase employees' feelings of autonomy, belongingness, and competence as a key to boost their high-quality motivation. This meant measuring the ABC and motivation before (T1) and after (T2), the intervention in order to capture benefits, calculating an ROI based on cost, and comparing actual Time2 impact to Time1 projections.

Step 1. Academic studies as well as market research have found that the total dollar value of what an employee was costing an organization per year could be approximated by twice the employee's annual base salary accounting for fringe benefits as well as a share of overhead cost, both in addition to base salary. If SmartCo's average base salary is doubled and multiplied by its number of employees, the total dollar value of the organization's workforce (based on cost) can be calculated at

Total Value per Employee = 2 × Base Salary = 2 × $50,000 = $100,000
Total Value of All Employees = Total Value per Employee × Number of Employees = $100,000 × 200
= $20,000,000

> where
> Total Value per Employee = total $ value of one employee at cost per year

Total Value of All Employees = total $ value of all employees at cost per year
BS = annual base salary ($50,000)
Number of employees = Number of employees (200)

"Going concern" is a key business principle in the preparation of financial accounts, suggesting a company or entity will be able to continue operating for a time (at least 12 months) sufficient to meet its commitments, obligations, and objectives. By applying the going concern principle to high-quality motivation it is suggested that, for any organization to sustain its operations, the $ value of engagement of its people cannot fall short of the $ value of employee cost on a continuous basis.

Expressed differently, employees' engagement needs to create at least, if not more, the $ value for an entity compared to the $ value of employees' total cost.

Three categories of employee engagement – engaged, disengaged, actively disengaged – are used and their definitions are adapted in terms of their value creation/destruction potential within the EVA model.

- Actively Disengaged employees do not produce any value; in fact, there is only cost.
- Disengaged employees produce value at the level of what they cost.
- Engaged employees produce more value beyond what they cost.

If the value creation should be at least the value of cost and assuming that disengaged employees create what they cost, engaged employees need to pick up all value that is being destroyed by actively disengaged employees in order for the going concern assumption to be fulfilled. That way, the value creation of each engaged employee at SmartCo can be calculated at

Incr_VC_per_Eng_Employee = (N_Act_Dis_Employees/N_Eng_Employees) x Total_Value_per_Employee
= (20/40) x $100,000 = $50,000
Total_VC_per_Eng_Employee = Total_Value_per_Employee + Incr_VC_per_Eng_Employee
= $100,000 + $50,000 = $150,000

> where
> Incr_VC_per_Eng_Employee = Incremental $ value created by each engaged employee beyond cost Total_VC_per_Eng_Employee = $ value created by each engaged employee
> Total_Value_per_Employee = total $ value of one employee at cost per year
> N_Act_Dis_Employees = number of actively disengaged employees N_Eng_Employees = number of engaged employees

Step 2. In a second step, the following question arises: If the engaged employees can create extra value at the level they do, why not also the disengaged and actively disengaged employees? That means there is a potential of foregone $ value that is not being created by having disengaged and actively disengaged people in the organization. This potential total foregone $ value, that is the total value creation potential at SmartCo, can be calculated at

PV_foregone = Incr_VC_per_Eng_Employee x NDisEmployees + Total_VC_per_Eng_Employee x N_Act_Dis_Employees
= $50,000 x 140 + $150,000 x 20
= $7.0m (disengaged PV) + $3.0m (actively disengaged PV)
= $10m (total PV)

> where
> PV_foregone = potential $ value foregone
> Incr_VC_per_Eng_Employee = Incremental $ value created by each engaged employee beyond cost Total_VC_per_Eng_Employee = $ value created by each engaged employee

NDisEmployees = number of disengaged employees
N_Act_Dis_Employees = number of actively disengaged employees

The above calculation shows the distribution of the value creation potential of PV_foregone ($10m). 70% ($7.0m) are at the level of disengaged employees and 30% ($3.0m) at the level of actively disengaged employees.

Step 3. Step 3 of the EVA model applies SDT's ABC principles of employees' perceived levels of autonomy, belongingness, and competence as drivers of their engagement. Autonomy, belongingness, and competence scores can be added together to compose a total ABC score. Statistical analyses of correlation and regression will provide the strength of links between the total ABC score and engagement.

SDT based research has consistently shown positive correlations of rxy between the ABC, employee engagement, and the potential foregone $ value. The potential value creation to be achieved by an intervention to increase employees' ABC scores at SmartCo through organizational design, training, and development can be calculated at

$$\text{Exp\_Eng\_Impact} = \text{rxy} \times \text{Exp\_Tns\_Impact} = 0.5 \times 10\% = 5\%$$

$$\text{Exp\_VC} = \text{Exp\_Eng\_Impact} \times \text{PV\_foregone} = 5\% \times \$10m = \$500,000$$

where
Exp_VC = expected $ value created by intervention
rxy = correlation between total ABC (TABC) and employee engagement in %

(i.e., if total need satisfaction increases by 100, employee engagement increases by rxy% from a statistical perspective, in this case 0.5 or 50%)

Exp_Tns_Impact = expected impact of intervention on total ABC (TABC) in %

(i.e., the intervention is expected to increase total ABC by Exp_Tns_Impact %, in this case 10%) Exp_Eng_Impact = expected impact of intervention on employee engagement in % (i.e., the intervention based expected increase in total ABC is expected to translate into an increase in employee engagement by Exp_Eng_Impact %, in this case 5%)

PV_foregone = potential foregone $ value

Step 4. The cost-benefit analysis of an individual measure, such as organizational design, training, or development, to increase employee engagement at SmartCo would give a return on investment (ROI_projected) of

$$ROI\_projected = Exp\_VC \,/\, Total\_Cost\_Intervention$$
$$= \$500{,}000 \,/\, \$350{,}000 = 142\%$$

where

Exp_VC = expected $ value created by intervention Total_Cost_Intervention = total $ cost of the intervention

Total_Cost_Intervention usually consists of two main items, change consultants' fees, and the cost of employees' time for attending workshops instead of performing their respective work roles. There may be cases where cost for building, construction, or travel need to be added. In the case of SmartCo, the cost of intervention was projected at $350,000 including consultants' fees and employees' time and travel expenses.

Step 5. After completion of the intervention, at T2, employees' ABC and engagement were surveyed again to capture actual impact compared to T1 levels and T1 projections. Actual engagement scores had increased by 12% (T2; from 4.1 to 4.6) instead of the projected 5% (T1); the ROI_actual was

$$Act\_VC = Act\_Eng\_Impact \times PV\_foregone$$
$$= 12\% \times \$10m = \$1,200,000$$

$$ROI\_actual = Act\_VC \text{ / } Total\_Cost\_Intervention$$
$$= \$1,200,000 \text{ / } \$350,000 = 342\%$$

> where
> Act_VC = Actual $ value created by intervention
> Act_Eng_Impact = Actual impact of intervention on employee engagement in % (in this case 12%)
> PV_foregone = potential foregone $ value Total_Cost_Intervention = total $ cost of the intervention

In summary, for every $1 invested in the intervention to increase employee engagement, the project returned $3.42 for SmartCo over a 12-month period. As a result of Thomas' intervention project, the Executive Committee saw a rise in several domains, such as SmartCo employees' calls to customers, customer satisfaction, sales and profits. On the other hand, work-related accidents, employee turnover, and absenteeism declined to an all-time low. The CEO had asked Thomas to show him the money, and Thomas did so by using the EVA model.

The EVA model represents a multi-disciplinary approach to cost-benefit analysis integrating best practices of organizational psychology, economics, accounting, and finance. EVA delivers conservative results due to its nature of a single period model (i.e., 12 months). However, the benefits of people investments do not abruptly stop after 12 months. There will be future benefits which can be included into an ROI calculation by discounting them back into the present. Of course, this will inflate the ROI number providing even more favorable results.

EVA can be applied to all facets of organizational design, training, and development. Any people investment in support of achieving desired behavioral outcomes can be modeled into EVA. In order to match other corporate investment proposals such as real estate, machinery, or branding, EVA can deliver ROI projections as well as actual ROIs after completion of a project. How to make projections? How do we know what benefits in terms of behavior and engagement a specific people investment will achieve? Well, how do marketing and sales forecast revenues for future years? And how do investment firms project cash flows from an equity participation investment? Experience is the answer! You have to use EVA in order to be able to make informed projections and decisions. The application of EVA is a skill that can be trained. For example, at SmartCo the projected increase in employee engagement was 5%. Actual results showed an increase of 12% after the intervention. EVA projections and actuals are company-culture specific. By using EVA consistently over time and in a variety of projects, users will become more proficient in terms of projecting outcomes, for example through internal benchmarking.

Since publication in 2019, EVA has been applied in practice in a variety of industries, in various countries. In the initial 2015 research study, researchers saw a projected T1 (12 months) ROI of 69.4% turn into an actual T2 ROI of 148.5% for the intervention project. This has been the most conservative, actual ROI for EVA's application in practice. In all other known cases, actual, 12-month ROIs were beyond 200%. In fact, in the case of SmartCo, the ROI was 342%. In conclusion, in a knowledge economy, investments in people may well be the most profitable corporate investments.

WHAT ABOUT YOU?

— Do you know how to do an ROI analysis on your people programs?
— Can your organization put such ROI/payback numbers on investments in employees?

- How can the calculation of ROI numbers help your organization to invest more effectively in high-quality employee motivation?

SUMMARY

It pays to take care of what is important, namely the ABC of motivation. Not only is it important in what the employees are experiencing daily but it is financially viable if you take the time and have the technique to calculate it.

Key References

Aelterman, N., Vansteenkiste, M., Haerens, L., Soenens, B., Fontaine, J.R.J., & Reeve, J. (2019). Toward an integrative and fine-grained insight in motivating and demotivating teaching styles: The merits of a circumplex approach. *Journal of Educational Psychology, 111*(3), 497-521.

Baard, P.P., Deci, E.L., & Ryan, R.M. (2004). Intrinsic need satisfaction: A motivational basis of performance and well-being in two work settings. *Journal of Applied Social Psychology, 34*, 2045-2068.

Bregman, R. (2021). Humankind: A Hopeful History. *Little, Brown and Company.*

Cerasoli, C.P., Nicklin, J.M., & Ford, M.T. (2014). Intrinsic motivation and extrinsic incentives jointly predict performance: A 40-year meta-analysis. *Psychological Bulletin, 140*(4), 980-1008.

Chen, B., Vansteenkiste, M., Beyers, W., Boone, L., Deci, E., van der Kaap-Deeder, J., Duriez, B., Lens, W., Matos, L., Mouratidis, T., Ryan, R., Sheldon, K., Soenens, B., Van Petegem, S., & Verstuyf, J. (2015). Basic psychological need satisfaction, need frustration, and need strength across four cultures.
Motivation and Emotion. 39(2), 216-236.

Deci, E.L., & Ryan, R.M. (2000). The "what" and "why" of goal pursuits: Human needs and the self-determination of behavior. *Psychological Inquiry, 11*(4), 227-268.

Deci, E.L., Olafsen, A.H., Ryan, R.M. (2017). Self-determination theory in work organizations: The state of a science. *Annual Review of Organizational Psychology and Organizational Behavior, 4*, 19-43.

Deci, E.L., Connell, J.P., & Ryan, R.M. (1989). Self-determination in a work organization. *Journal of Applied Psychology, 74*, 580-590.

Deci, E.L., Ryan, R.M., Gagné, M., Leone, D., Usunov, J., & Kornazheva, B. (2001). Need Satisfaction, Motivation, and Well-Being in the Work Organizations of a Former Eastern Bloc Country: A Cross-Cultural Study of Self-Determination. *Personality and Social Psychology Bulletin, 27*, 930-942.

Demerouti, E., Bakker, A.B., Nachreiner, F., & Schaufeli, W.B. (2001). The job demands-resources model of burnout. *Journal of Applied Psychology, 86*(3), 499-512.

Derue, D.S., Nahrgang, J.D., Wellman, N., & Humphrey, S.E. (2011). Trait and behavioral theories of leadership: An integration and meta-analytic test of their relative validity. *Personnel Psychology, 64*(1), 7-52.

Forest, J., Gilbert, M.H., Beaulieu, G., & Le Brock, P. (2014). In M. Gagné (ed.), *Translating research results in economic terms: An application of economic utility analysis using SDT-based interventions. The Oxford Handbook of Work Engagement, Motivation, and Self-Determination Theory* (pp. 335-346). Oxford: Oxford University Press.

Gagné, M., & Forest, J. (2008). The study of compensation systems through the lens of self-determination theory: Reconciling 35 years of debate. *Canadian Psychology, 49*, 225-232.

Gagné, M., Forest, J., Vansteenkiste, M., Crevier-Braud, L., Van den Broeck, A., Aspeli, A.K., ..., Westbye, C. (2015). The multidimensional work motivation scale: Validation evidence in seven languages and nine countries. *European Journal of Work and Organizational Psychology, 24(2)*, 178-196.

Grant, A.M. (2008). The significance of task significance: Job performance effects, relational mechanisms, and boundary conditions. *Journal of Applied Psychology, 93(1)*, 108-124.

Howard, J.L., Gagné, M., Morin, A.J., & Forest, J. (2018). Using Bifactor Exploratory Structural Equation Modeling to Test for a Continuum Structure of Motivation. *Journal of Management, 44(7)*, 2638-2664.

Howard, J., Gagné, M., Morin, A.J.S., & Van den Broeck, A. (2016). Motivation profiles at work: A self-determination theory approach. *Journal of Vocational Behavior, 95*, 74-89.

Jungert, T., Van den Broeck, A., Schreurs, B., & Osterman, U. (2018). How colleagues can support each other's needs and motivation: An intervention on employee work motivation. *Applied Psychology, 67(1)*, 3-29.

Kuvaas, B., Buch, R., Gagné, M., & Dysvik, A. (2016). Do you get what you pay for? Sales incentives and implications for motivation and changes in turnover intention and work effort. *Motivation and Emotion, 40*, 667-680.

Landry, T., Zhang, A., Papaschristopoulos, Y., & Forest, J. (2020). Applying self-determination theory to understand the motivational impact of cash rewards: New evidence from lab experiments. *International Journal of Psychology, 55(3)*, 487-498.

Manganelli, L., & Forest, J. (2020). Using Self-Determination Theory to Understand when and how Money Buys Happiness: a Cross-Sectional and Intervention Study. *Applied Research in Quality of Life*. 1-26.

Moreau, E., & Mageau, G. A. (2012). The importance of perceived autonomy support for the psychological health and work satisfaction of health professionals: Not only supervisors count, colleagues too!. *Motivation and Emotion, 36*, 268-286.

Mueller, M. (2019). Show me the money: Toward an economic model for a cost-benefit analysis of employee engagement interventions. *International Journal of Organization Theory and Behavior, 22(1)*, 43-64.

Mueller, M.B., & Lovell, G. (2018). Senior executives' basic psychological need, satisfaction and psychological well-being: Is it different at the top? *Management and Economics Research Journal, 4*, 289-304.

Olafsen, A.H., Halvari, H., Forest, J., & Deci, E.L. (2015). Show them the money? The role of pay, autonomy support, and justice in a self-determination theory model of intrinsic work motivation.

Scandinavian Journal of Psychology, 56(4), 447-457.

Parker, S.K., Andrei, D.M., & Van den Broeck, A. (2019). Poor work design begets poor work design: Capacity and willingness antecedents of individual work design behavior. *Journal of Applied Psychology, 104(7)*, 907-928.

Rosenberg, M.B. (2011). *Geweldloze communicatie*. Lemniscaat.

Ryan, R.M., & Deci, E.L. (2017). *Self-determination theory: Basic psychological needs in motivation, development, and wellness*. New York: Guilford Publishing.

Slemp, G.R., Kern, M. L., Patrick, K.J., & Ryan, R.M. (2018b). Leader autonomy support in the workplace: A meta-analytic review. *Motivation and Emotion, 42*(5), 706-724.

Trépanier, S.-G., Forest, J., Fernet, C., & Austin, S. (2015). On the psychological and motivational processes linking job characteristics to employee functioning: Insights from self-determination theory. *Work and Stress, 29*, 286-305.

Van den Broeck, A., Ferris, D. L., Chang, C.-H., & Rosen, C. C. (2016). A review of self-determination theory's basic psychological needs at work. *Journal of Management, 42*(5), 1195-1229.

Van den Broeck, A., Lens, W., De Witte, H., & Van Coillie, H. (2013). Unraveling the importance of the quantity and the quality of workers' motivation for well-being: A person-centered perspective. *Journal of Vocational Behavior, 82*(1), 69-78.

Van den Broeck, A., Vansteenkiste, M., De Witte, H., & Lens, W. (2008). Explaining the relationships between job characteristics, burnout, and engagement: The role of basic psychological need satisfaction. *Work & Stress, 22*(3), 277-294.

Van den Broeck, A., Vansteenkiste, M., De Witte, H., & Soenens, B. (2010). Capturing autonomy, competence, and relatedness at work: Construction and initial validation of the Work-related Basic Need Satisfaction scale. *Journal of Occupational and Organizational Psychology, 83*, 981-1002.

Vansteenkiste, M., Neyrinck, B., Niemiec, C.P., Soenens, B., De Witte H., & Van den Broeck, A. (2007). On the relations among work value orientations, psychological need satisfaction and job outcomes: A self-determination theory approach. *Journal of Occupational and Organizational Psychology, 80*, 251-277.

Printed and bound by CPI Group (UK) Ltd, Croydon, CR0 4YY

25/03/2025

14647324-0002